AMERICA vs. AMERICA

A Manifesto for the American Woman

QUAN JAMEL FORT

PAGE PUBLISHING, INC.
Conneaut Lake, PA

First originally published by Page Publishing 2020

ISBN 978-1-68456-960-1 (pbk)
ISBN 978-1-68456-961-8 (digital)

Printed in the United States of America

In loving memory to my aunt, Patricia Ann Pierce-LaCaprara, who was viciously murdered on Monday, July 8, 2013.

To my grandmother, Beverly Jeanne Bailey-Pierce, who died of old age on Thursday, June 12, 2014.

To all victims of domestic violence.

CONTENTS

Introduction

I was born on May 21, 1990. I attended public schools in the Binghamton and Susquehanna Valley School Districts where I experienced racially motivated bullying. On top of that, I had to endure eighteen years of psychological, verbal, and economic abuse at the hands of my mother's abusive boyfriend. I got the idea for this manifesto in 2008 during the Great Recession and Barack Obama's first presidential election. That is when I began the first draft of this manifesto. It was these two events that inspired my interest in politics. I registered to vote as soon as I turned eighteen. On Sunday, June 28, 2009, I graduated from Binghamton High School. In August 2009, I entered Broome Community College as a business administration major. At BCC, I met Julia, a Filipina American, who was also a business administration major. During the two semesters that I have known her (Fall 2009 / Spring 2010), I learned very little about her personally but did develop an interest in Filipina women. I am now extremely selective in my search for a life partner, with Asian American among the qualities I look for. In August 2011, I began attending Broome Community College as a liberal arts major. This was more in line with my political interests. This is also when I made the decision to eventually go to law school and study environmental law. I was also called to serve as an alternate juror in Broome County Court. In January 2013, my mother's abusive boyfriend sued my mother for "damages" in claims court. At this point, he was no longer living with us. My mother countersued and on the day of the court case, he never showed up and my mother won. On Monday, July 8, 2013, my aunt, Patricia Ann Pierce-LaCaprara, was viciously murdered. On June 12, 2014, my grandmother, Beverly Jeanne Bailey-Pierce, died. After years of unemployment, I wrote my five-year plan at the beginning of 2016 that included finding employment. So far, I have worked for American Food & Vending, Compass Group, and Price Chopper.

The purpose of this manifesto is to give you a nonpartisan understanding of the American two-party political system. After doing research in psychology and history, I felt as though the only way to provide that kind of understanding was to get down to the personal level of individual Americans. As an only child with no siblings, I realized I was the only one among members of my immediate family. In the first part of this book, "The Conflict Between the Siblings," I describe the behavior of each sibling in the birth order. In the second and third parts, "The Extroverted Personality" and "The Introverted Personality," I describe the two major personality types developed by each sibling as a result of their behaviors toward each other. In the fourth part, "The Influence of Personality on Politics," I describe the politics of the left wing and right wing, the four different political views—liberal, conservative, progressive, and reactionary—a list of currently debated political issues, and bring it all together with a parable.

As part of my theory, I apply each political issue to the personality type that I believe it most fits. The next part is to then apply all this to historical people and events in the fifth part, "How Personal Politics Has Influenced Twentieth- and Twenty-First-Century Decision-Making." In the last part, "A Theory Explaining Our Current Political Situation," I explain my theory. This manifesto is not easy reading. As you read through each section, you have to really pay attention. Look back if you have to. Also, this is not an anti-sibling manifesto. In the nineteenth and early twentieth centuries, there were very few only-borns, aside from President Franklin Delano Roosevelt and newspaper mogul William Randolph Hearst. I will discuss the personality of only-borns in another book later on.

You will also notice that I emphasize on segregation and discrimination in the United States, *past* and *present*, particularly African American racial segregation and discrimination. I will let you know that I myself am African American on my father's side and also a male feminist, so there should be no false accusations of me being "racist" or "sexist." When I talk about fundamentalist Christians and their beliefs, I am only referring to a particular group of Christians and not Christians in general. In the section "<u>How Personal Politics Has Influenced Twentieth- and Twenty-First-Century Decision-Making</u>," I keep historical events centered on the United States.

When I talk about World War II, I won't go into detail about Adolf Hitler and his rise to power. I will just talk about key events, such as the entrance of the Allied powers and the atomic bombings of Japan. When I talk about the Vietnam War, I won't go into detail about Ho Chi Minh and the Viet Cong's rise to power but instead keep the focus on United States' involvement. I won't give my personal opinion or discuss in much detail, controversial issues such as abortion, same-sex marriage, and separation of church and state. I won't talk about political scandals such as Watergate and Monica Lewinsky.

THE CONFLICT BETWEEN THE SIBLINGS

The firstborn, because they are used to get their parents' undivided attention before the second child's birth, are constantly striving to keep their parents' attention. They do this by conforming to their parents' rules in order to please their parents, but they will misbehave if they fail. They believe they are superior to their younger sibling or siblings and that as the eldest they are always right about everything. They will feel neglected when the second child is born.

The second born has a more advanced sibling ahead of him/her so they never have their parents' undivided attention and will act as though they are in a race with the firstborn. They don't always like their position in the family and may rebel and push down their other siblings. They will also either feel in a state of uncertainty about their own abilities if the first child is successful or be successful if the first child fails.

The middle born in a family of three siblings doesn't have the "rights" of the oldest or the "privileges" of the youngest and may feel that life is unfair to them and that they don't have a place in the family. They may feel unloved and left out as well. He/she may become a problem child and push down their other siblings in order to elevate themselves. In large families, there are more children in the middle who must learn to cooperate to get what they want because their parents can't always give to each child all at the same time. As such, they learn to adapt and are able to deal with the oldest and youngest sibling.

The youngest born feels inferior and tries to overtake their older siblings. They always remain "the baby" of the family even though they may feel small and weak. In a family of three, the youngest may ally with his/her older sibling against his/her middle sibling.

Every sibling in the birth order, whether firstborn, second born, middle child or children, or youngest born, develops a personality composed of the "big 5" aspects of <u>extroversion</u>, <u>agreeableness</u>, <u>conscientiousness</u>, <u>neuroticism</u>, and <u>openness</u>.

The Extroverted Personality

1. People make friends quickly and can form close, intimate relationships.
2. They like companionship and associating with other extroverts.
3. They are group leaders who like to speak out and take charge as they direct other people's activities.
4. They are involved in numerous activities.
5. They are thrill seekers and risk-takers who love hustle and bustle and bright lights.
6. For them, happiness, joy, and enthusiasm are experienced on a daily basis.
7. They are highly trusting of all people whom they believe are honest, fair, trustworthy and have good intentions.
8. They are open, honest, direct, truthful, and trustworthy as they proceed from genuine feelings.
9. They are concerned for other people's welfare.
10. In order to get along with others, they will compromise their own needs.
11. They moderately estimate their own talents and abilities.
12. They feel the pain of others because they are compassionate.
13. They feel they have common sense, drive, and self-control which they believe is necessary for achieving success.
14. They live according to routines and schedules and are plan makers and list keepers.
15. They have a strong sense of moral obligation.

16. They strive to be recognized as successful and have a strong sense of direction in life.
17. They overcome their reluctance to start tasks and are able to stay on track.
18. When making decisions, they take their time.
19. They may be fearful in some situations and feel nervous, uneasiness, and anxious.
20. They are bitter and resentful when they feel cheated by someone because they are sensitive about being fairly treated.
21. They may have difficulty beginning activities because they lack the energy to do so.
22. They may have unrealistic and exaggerated fears of others making fun of them and are shy and uncomfortable around people.
23. They may not use their full mental capacity and will be focused on short-term pleasures and rewards instead of long-term consequences.
24. They may feel helpless, confused, and panicking when they are under stress.
25. In order to create a more interesting world, they use fantasy.
26. Most extroverts may not be artistically trained or talented, but they are interested in natural and artificial beauty.
27. They have good awareness of their own feelings.
28. They find routine and long association with something boring.
29. They are open to new and unusual ideas and enjoy puzzles, riddles, and brainteasers.
30. They are psychological liberals who challenge authority, accepted standards, behavior, and traditional values. Some even extend it further and are unfriendly and antagonistic toward rules, feel pity and sorrow for lawbreakers, and love complete disorder, confusion, and unpredictable behavior. They have a tendency to lean toward liberal politics.

This comprises one part of a personality that a person possesses. The other "big 5" aspects are <u>introversion</u>, <u>disagreeableness</u>, <u>carelessness</u>, <u>unneroticism</u>, and <u>narrow-mindedness</u>.

THE INTROVERTED PERSONALITY

1. People are very far-off and slow to reveal emotions, opinions and don't make friends as easily.
2. They are not hostile toward other people but they do avoid large crowds and have great need for alone time by themselves.
3. They let the more extroverted control group activities and talk very little themselves.
4. They follow a slower and relaxed pace.
5. They are not thrill seekers and are buried beneath too much noise and disturbance.
6. They are unlikely to feel positive emotions.
7. They will sometimes see others as selfish, dangerous, and showing a use of dishonest tactics.
8. They will deceive some truth in a social relationship if necessary.
9. People who request help are treated as though they are imposing as the introvert does not like to help people in need.
10. They will frighten others to get their way.
11. They are seen by others as arrogant because they often describe themselves as superior.
12. They pride themselves for making reasonable judgments without being influenced by opinions or personal feelings.
13. They are more concerned with truth and treating all rivals fair and just rather than forgiveness.

14. They may feel they are not in control of their lives and become thrown in random directions and unable to efficiently plan their own activities.
15. They can be seen as unreliable and irresponsible because they view contracts, rules, and regulations over confining.
16. They are seen as lazy because they prefer to do only minor work.
17. They procrastinate and fail to complete tasks they want to complete.
18. Without thinking of alternatives and possible consequences, they will do the first thing they can think of.
19. They are without fear and calm.
20. They do not get angry easily.
21. They are free from depressive feelings.
22. In social situations, they do not feel nervous.
23. They do not have the urge to overindulge themselves and don't experience cravings that are hard to resist.
24. They are clear-thinking, confident, and self-assured when they are stressed.
25. They prefer facts over fantasy.
26. They lack interest in the arts and sciences.
27. They don't openly express their emotions because they are less aware of their feelings.
28. They prefer routines that are familiar to them and are uncomfortable with change.
29. They see intellectual exercises as a waste of time and prefer to deal with people and things instead of ideas.
30. They are psychological conservatives who prefer the security and stableness that compliance with tradition brings. They have a tendency to lean toward conservative politics.

THE INFLUENCE OF PERSONALITY ON POLITICS

1. In politics, there is the left wing and the right wing.
2. The left is composed of liberals and social democrats, state capitalists, socialists and communists, and anarchists.
3. The right is composed of conservatives and corporate capitalists, corporatists, fascists, and Nazis, monarchists and religious fundamentalists, and autocratic despots.

First of all, you need to understand that, on the right, there is a big difference between a <u>conservative</u> and a <u>reactionary</u>. A conservative <u>doesn't</u> want anything to change. They are happy with society as it is, presently, and persist on keeping it that way. A reactionary <u>does</u> want change but instead of moving society forward, they want society to go backward. An example of a reactionary would be Fascist Italy's Benito Mussolini who wanted to "restore" Italy back to the days of the Roman Empire. Adolf Hitler was both a reactionary and a revolutionary. On the left, there is also a big difference between a <u>liberal</u> and a <u>progressive</u>. Liberals are <u>revolutionary</u> and expect total and complete change within a very short period of time. Progressives are <u>reformers</u> who believe change will come by simply improving the existing society through legislation. The Occupy Wall Street and Black Lives Matter Movements are examples of revolutionary movements. The Tea Party Movement is an example of a <u>reactionary</u> movement. Most politicians in office who call themselves "liberal" are, in fact, "progressives," and the same is true for the other side of politicians who call themselves "conservatives" who are, in fact, "reactionaries."

The current issues in politics are <u>abortion</u>, <u>same-sex marriage</u>, <u>separation of church and state</u>, <u>undocumented immigration</u>, <u>global warming</u>, <u>social welfare programs</u>, <u>gun control</u>, <u>the United Nations</u>, <u>euthanasia</u>, <u>health care</u>, <u>Social Security</u>, <u>national defense</u>, <u>economy</u>, <u>embryonic stem cell research</u>, <u>affirmative action</u>, <u>education</u>, <u>the death penalty</u>, <u>terrorism</u>, <u>energy</u>, <u>taxes</u>, <u>private property</u>, and <u>Homeland Security</u>.

1. <u>Liberals</u> see abortion as a woman's right.
   <u>Conservatives</u> see abortion as murder.
2. <u>Liberals</u> define *marriage* as an "institution between two people in love."
   <u>Conservatives</u> define *marriage* as an "institution between a man and a woman."
3. <u>Liberals</u> believe church and government should be completely separate.
   <u>Conservatives</u> believe the government should promote public religious expression.
4. <u>Liberals</u> believe immigration laws should allow automatic citizenship to all undocumented immigrants.
   <u>Conservatives</u> believe immigration laws should deport all undocumented immigrants.
5. <u>Liberals</u> believe global warming is the single greatest threat to humanity.
   <u>Conservatives</u> believe global warming is a fairy tale.
6. <u>Liberals</u> believe social welfare programs help the poor.
   <u>Conservatives</u> believe social welfare programs promote laziness.
7. <u>Liberals</u> believe only the police and military need guns.
   <u>Conservatives</u> believe everyone needs a gun or guns.
8. <u>Liberals</u> believe America should give all authority to the United Nations.
   <u>Conservatives</u> believe America should withdraw from the United Nations.
9. <u>Liberals</u> support euthanasia and believe the terminally ill have a right to die.

<u>Conservatives</u> believe euthanasia is physician-assisted suicide.

10. <u>Liberals</u> believe everyone should have universal health care. <u>Conservatives</u> believe everyone should have employer-provided health care.

11. <u>Liberals</u> believe Social Security should be protected. <u>Conservatives</u> believe Social Security should become private.

12. <u>Liberals</u> want to decrease military spending. <u>Conservatives</u> want to increase military spending.

13. <u>Liberals</u> believe the government should regulate the economy. <u>Conservatives</u> believe the economy should be unregulated.

14. <u>Liberals</u> support embryonic stem cell research. <u>Conservatives</u> think embryonic stem cell research is wrong because it requires a human fetus killed.

15. <u>Liberals</u> believe affirmative action promotes racial equality. <u>Conservatives</u> believe affirmative action promotes reverse discrimination.

16. <u>Liberals</u> believe public schools are the best way to education the future population. <u>Conservatives</u> believe homeschooling and religious schools should educate the future population.

17. <u>Liberals</u> believe the death penalty is the wrong punishment for murder. <u>Conservatives</u> believe the death penalty fits the crime of murder.

18. <u>Liberals</u> believe terrorists should be treated like human beings with civil rights. <u>Conservatives</u> believe terrorists should be stripped of all rights.

19. <u>Liberals</u> believe energy policy should focus on renewable sources only. <u>Conservatives</u> believe energy policy should focus mainly on nonrenewable sources.

20. <u>Liberals</u> want to increase taxes for the wealthy.

<u>Conservatives</u> want to decrease taxes for the wealthy.
21. <u>Liberals</u> support the government's right to take private property for public use by paying the owner for it (eminent domain).
<u>Conservatives</u> believe eminent domain is wrong in cases involving private development.
22. <u>Liberals</u> support random screening.
<u>Conservatives</u> support racial profiling.

To make sense of all this, I will tell you a story that I call "the Parable of the Two Conductors." Imagine a train consisting of a steam locomotive and fifty cars trailing along behind. You're a passenger on this train and you look out the window and see a magnificent site: trees, grass, blue sky, mountains, river, a small village opposite side of the river, a few boats on the river, etc. However, on the inside of the train, in the car you are seated, you see children running up and down the aisle. In the seat next to you, there is an overly obese passenger snoring loudly and it is very annoying to you. Directly behind you is a passenger who is constantly talking on her cell phone, yelling, cursing, and whatever else at the person she is talking to. The passenger in front of you is an annoying preacher type who keeps on standing up in his seat every so often to persistently preach the "good news" about Jesus and the Second Coming, as if you haven't already heard it before. Across the aisle, you see a passenger minding her own business, sitting by the window, and reading her book. In your mind, you try to stay calm but you just want to pull your hair out. Then you begin to notice that the train is slowing down in the middle of a barren desert. Two conductors have entered the car. They don't really explain the problem but just try to calm everyone down by saying, "Everything will be all right."

Then they leave the car, bickering and arguing, and the moment they do, all hell breaks loose and the passengers begin fistfighting each other over the stupidest things that have nothing to do with the current situation. Up at the front of the train, in the locomotive, the engineer just cannot figure out what is going on ether. The engine suddenly gave out, bringing the entire train to a halt. The two conductors, one wearing a red jacket and the other a blue jacket, have entered the locomotive, still bickering and arguing. When the engineer cannot explain the problem and has no solution to fix it, the conductors decide to replace him with a new engineer. But the conductors begin bickering over choosing a new engineer. Both conductors want to choose an engineer from among the passengers but the blue jacket conductor wants an engineer chosen from the left side of the train while the red jacket conductor wants an engineer chosen from the right side of the train. Ever since the train left the original terminal, the two conductors have been competing to get as many passengers on the train as possible. The blue jacket conductor brings on passengers from the left side of the train that consists of single women, homosexuals, atheists, undocumented immigrants, environmentalists, feminists, civil rights leaders, labor union leaders, etc. The red jacket conductor brings on passengers from the right side of the train that consists of racists, chauvinists, xenophobes (stranger fearers), wealthy businessmen, corporate CEOs, etc. The train has become so overcrowded that both conductors had to separate the two sides and, in so doing, have caused the two sides to hate each other. The passengers on the train have now gotten to the point where they are divided on their destination.

The left side passengers want their blue jacket conductor to choose a new engineer from their side. They want the train to keep going forward and pick up more passengers from the left side of the train. They want to take over the whole train and push the right side passengers and their conductor off. The right side passengers want their red jacket conductor to choose a new engineer from their side. They want the train to go back to the original terminal. They want to push the left side passengers and their conductor off and then take over the train and move along toward a destination of their choosing. Here is where you come in. You are seated in the middle of the train and that means you are not on the left or the right side of the train. It also means you are not among those who are under ether the blue jacket or the red jacket conductor. You get up and walk your way down the aisle and into the next car and you keep walking until you reach the locomotive. Once at the locomotive, you notice that the coal car is half empty, the engineer and the fireman have disappeared, and the two conductors are standing outside the locomotive, bickering and arguing. You decide to go back and persuade all the passengers to rise up and take over the train.

1. The extroverted personality can be closely identified with those who support modern liberal political views.

2. Extroverts are group-centered and emphasize the collective interests of the group rather than the individual interests of its members. Liberal policies are based on making the individual dependent on the group and submissive to group interests.

3. Extroverts view established corporations and wealthy individuals with contempt so their liberal policies use "wealth redistribution" as a way of taking away their excessive wealth by force and give it to those who don't have it and feel entitled to it, even though they did not earn it. They do this through high taxes, directed at the wealthy, which are supposed to help pay for things like social welfare programs, universal health care, social security, and public education. Extroverts emphasize government regulation to weaken the power of the individual and the individual's ability to make a living without group assistance.

4. Extroverts see no reason to defend themselves or the group against aggressors because, in their view, everyone is a good person, even hard-core terrorists who have been misguided by his or her life experiences can be rehabilitated and placed back into society. Extroverts support liberal policies that advocate very strict gun control laws, at the national level, seeking to take away a person's right to own weapons, to decrease spending on the military, to abolish the death penalty for convicted murderers, and to give compassionate treatment to terrorists and criminals.

5. Extroverts want individuals to downplay their own intelligence, talents, and abilities. They support liberal "education" policies that emphasize "collective learning" in

public schools using a mandatory curriculum that forces students to "learn" collectively in groups that are referred to as "classes."

6. Extroverts use fantasy and are interested in beauty that is both natural and artificial and are open to new and creative ideas. Extroverts support liberal policies that emphasize a more equal and tolerant world. They support an affirmative action policy that focuses mainly on single women, homosexual couples and their right to get married, atheists and their right to reject God, undocumented immigrants and their right to gain citizenship, some Jews, some Arabs and Muslims, some Hispanics, some Asians, and some African Americans. They support liberal policies that emphasize the need for renewable sources of energy and to conserve the remaining nonrenewable sources of energy. Extroverts use Hollywood and the left wing media (CBS, NBC, ABC, PBS, CNN, etc.) to promote their political views as propaganda to the general public.

7. Extroverts believe that all nations on earth should unite under a single world political system, economy, culture, society, etc. They support a foreign policy that emphasizes the need for the United Nations to act as a "world government."

8. The Introverted Personality can be closely identified with those who support modern conservative political views.

9. Introverts are individual-centered and emphasize their own individual interests rather than the collective interests of the group. Conservative policies are based on empowering the individual and making the group dependent on the individual and submissive to individual interests.

10. Introverts view the government and government bureaucrats with contempt so their conservative policies emphasize low taxes, a deregulated economy, private social security, employer-provided health care, and private education in religious schools and homeschooling. They favor the private power of corporations, which under the law are

individual "persons," that have the right to sue and be sued in their own name. Introverts believe that corporations are "individuals" in their own right and that society should be organized into "corporate groups," parents and children, teachers and students, management and workers, preachers and congregants, etc., each with different levels of hierarchy and with the former leading the latter.

11. Introverts see violence and danger in society and that individuals have to be ready to defend themselves against potential aggressors. Introverts support conservative policies that advocate the right to have weapons, increased spending on the military, the death penalty for convicted murderers, and to strip terrorists and criminals of their civil rights and liberties.

12. Introverts emphasize the need for religion and order to give their lives meaning, purpose, and structure. Introverts want individuals to subject themselves to a "higher power" and follow a strict moral code. Introverts tend to be more serious about their religious beliefs and attend Bible, Quran, Torah, etc. study groups in order to understand their religion in its entirety, unlike extroverts who attend church simply because other people are there or use their "faith" as a way of bringing others into their church but have very little understanding of church doctrine.

13. Introverts prefer the real world of facts over fantasy, have no interests in the arts and sciences, and view intellectual exercises as a waste of time. They prefer dealing with people and things instead of ideas. Introverts support conservative policies that emphasize preserving the established order. They oppose affirmative action on the grounds that it promoted "reverse discrimination." They believe global warming is not caused by human activities and support conservative policies that emphasize continuing the use of nonrenewable sources of energy such as oil, coal, nuclear, and natural gas. Introverts use talk-radio and the right

wing media (Fox News) to promote their political views as propaganda to the general public.

14. Introverts believe the United States and other countries are separate countries and should remain separate. They support conservative policies that emphasize treating other countries different from each other and withdrawing from the United Nations.

How Personal Politics Has Influenced Twentieth- and Twenty-First-Century Decision-Making

The American frontier began in the eighteenth century with the Alleghany Mountains. In the early nineteenth century, the Mississippi River was the frontier, followed by the Missouri River in the mid-nineteenth century. The Rocky Mountains and dry Southwestern lands became the frontier of the late nineteenth century. The American frontier can be divided into the Native American trader's frontier, the rancher's frontier, and the farmer's frontier. Let's start with the frontier of the Native American traders who used the Indian trails that were once the buffalo trails. The Indian trails became roads, then toll roads called turnpikes and then railroads. There were Native American villages along the Indian trails where trading posts were eventually located. Cities like Albany, Pittsburgh, Detroit, Chicago, St. Louis, Kansas City, and Council Bluffs grew from these trading posts. The frontier of the ranchers was so remote, it lacked the necessary transportation and therefore had to be extended rapidly so that a cattle raiser could bring his product to the market with ease. The frontier of the farmers had been obstructed by Native American resistance, the location of passes and river valleys, the unequal forces of lands that were fertile and situated in favorable locations, army posts, and salt springs. The frontier army post was a center for western settlement and the government determined settlement lines through expeditions conducted by both explorers and military personnel. Salt springs were necessary for the earliest frontier settlers who required salt for preserving meats. They were discovered near the Kanawha and Holston Rivers, as well as in Kentucky and central New York. The settlers were no longer dependent on the East Coast for salt and were able to settle beyond the mountains. Lands were settled over time through a series of waves, beginning with the pioneer farmer, followed by the immigrant farmer, and finally the industrial capitalists. The English indentured servants, the Scotch-Irish, and the Pennsylvania Germans moved out west and eventually were merged into a mixed race. This produced a unique American nationality. As settlers moved farther out west, we became more independent from England and merchants were high in demand on the East Coast. Railroad legislation, protective tariffs, and disposing public lands were improvements to the interior that influenced federal legislation. The Louisiana Purchase was a result of the demands of the frontier. The Middle Colonies was more diverse and less English then the South and New England and had more in common with the frontier. The frontier produced individualism and in return, individualism promoted democracy. Democracy, on the other hand, has its negative side effects such as individual selfishness, unlimited individual liberty, and intolerance of education and administrative experience. George Washington, Thomas Jefferson, James Madison, and Thomas Benton all wanted to limit frontier expansion. Religious denominations and colleges were established in the west by people from New England, Pennsylvania, New York, and Maryland. Rival churches and universities began to compete against each other for congregants and students among the frontier residents. The frontier ended with the Oklahoma Territory. It was formerly known as Indian Territory but had been opened to white settlers beginning with a rush an 1889, 1891, and 1892. The largest rush was that of the Cherokee Strip Land Run in 1893, in which Fred Sutton was among them. A lottery was used to determine the rush of 1901 and in 1906 the general public was allowed to settle whatever land was leftover.

In applying this to my extrovert/introvert theory, I would have to say that the white settlers were the extroverts. They didn't want the same old routine of living on the Atlantic coast and keeping the United States confined to the boundary line of the Appalachian Mountains or the Mississippi River. They were free as Americans and they wanted to enjoy their freedom by moving out west. They wanted a new start and to see new landscapes. The Native Americans were the introverts. They preferred to remain on their ancestral lands and live their traditional lifestyles and although some did convert to Christianity and "civilize" themselves, like the Cherokee, Choctaw, Chickasaw, Creek, and Seminole tribes, others were more resistant and were willing to fight to defend themselves and their land against the white settlers and the US government. The more hostile tribes were uncomfortable with the changes made to their sacred lands by white settlements and the railroads. These Native American tribes fought a series of "Indian wars" against the US government.

Thomas Edison invented the phonograph (record player) and the incandescent light bulb while George Westinghouse invented the railway air brake. Westinghouse and Edison would eventually be brought face-to-face in a "battle of the currents" to see who would succeed in bringing electricity to the general population of the United States, and to a greater extent, the world. Thomas Edison and his researchers at Menlo Park were pushing for direct current (DC) electricity that produces low voltage currents through the use of several power plants in a single city. One of Thomas Edison's researchers was Nikola Tesla, who disagreed on direct current (DC) electricity and proposed the high voltage alternating current (AC) electricity that uses transmission lines carrying electricity from a single power plant, several miles away, to substations where the voltage is lowered and lowered again near the consumer. Nikola Tesla was unable to come to an agreement with his employer, Thomas Edison, over alternating current (AC) electricity. He quit and eventually became employed with George Westinghouse who accepted Tesla's AC electricity after solving many of the problems associated with it. Thomas Edison still wanted his DC electricity to be the dominant form of electricity and set out to prove to the people that AC electricity is dangerous. He went so far as to push the New York State Legislature to pass a law making electrocution a form of capital punishment, allowing convicted murderer William Kemmler to be the first person executed in this manner in a Westinghouse AC electric chair. Thomas Edison promoted his DC electricity as providing electricity to the population using small distribution companies that would be subjected to local laws, not large corporations. George Westinghouse promoted AC electricity as providing electricity to the population using grids. His AC electrical grids would allow both cities and rural areas to benefit, unlike Thomas Edison's DC electrical distribution companies that would only benefit cities and leave rural areas still dependent on kerosene. In 1893, George Westinghouse won his first contract to power the Columbian Exposition World Fair and his second contract to turn Niagara Falls into a power plant, generating electricity for the entire Northeast. George Westinghouse might have won the "battle of the currents," with AC as the dominant form of electricity, but we use Thomas Edison's incandescent light bulbs to bring electric light into our homes and businesses. In 1891, Thomas Edison patented the kinetograph and the kinetoscope. The former would be used to capture a series of images on film and the latter would play them back. Thomas Edison and one of his researchers, William Kennedy Laurie Dickson disagreed on whether the kinetoscope or another type of projector should be used. With the kinetoscope, viewers could only see the film one person at a time while Dickson's idea was to allow multiple people to see the film at once on a large screen. Unable to come to an agreement, as with Nikola Tesla and electricity, Dickson left to work for a competing company. John D. Rockefeller formed Standard Oil in 1863 as an oil refining company which he incorporated in 1870. In 1877, Tom Scott of the Pennsylvania Railroad and Joseph Potts of the Empire Transportation Company hatched a plan to buy oil refineries and ship their contents over Pennsylvania and Empire rail lines. In return, John D. Rockefeller teamed up with both the New York Central Railroad and the Erie Railroad. He cancelled Standard Oil's shipping contract with the Pennsylvania Railroad and where Standard Oil competed with the Empire Transportation Company, he slashed his kerosene prices. At John D. Rockefeller's request, the New York Central Railroad and the Erie Railroad cut the rates of their freight and continued doing so to match the rates of the Pennsylvania Railroad and the Empire Transportation Company. In order to make it so that Standard Oil would not have to ship oil on the rail lines owned by the Pennsylvania Railroad, John D. Rockefeller closed down Standard Oil's Pittsburgh refineries. Eventually, after economic instability, worker walkouts, angry mobs, and violence in the streets, Tom Scott and Joseph Potts were left with no other choice but to sell out to Standard Oil. John D. Rockefeller then organized a trust in 1882 in which a board of trustees controlled the small entities of Standard Oil. As a result of a New Jersey law passed in 1888 and widened in 1889, 1893, and 1896 that involved holding companies, John D. Rockefeller was able to charter the Standard Oil Company of New Jersey in 1899.

Andrew Carnegie bought out the Pittsburgh Bessemer Steel Works company in 1883 and hired a ruthless businessman named Henry Clay Frick as chairman. Andrew Carnegie made a temporary truce with the Amalgamated Association of Iron and Steel Workers labor union in 1889. Carnegie Steel was formed in 1892. His methods were focused on cutting costs rather than simply producing profits, which he believed would take care of themselves. He preferred to use the most modern equipment available at the time for manufacturing his steel. The year (1892) was the year of three key events that dramatically and suddenly changed the steel industry and its workers. First, Andrew Carnegie goes on a vacation in his homeland of Scotland and leaves Henry Frick in charge. Second, Pittsburgh Bessemer Steel Works company merges with two other Carnegie-owned businesses to form the Carnegie Steel Company. The workers of the new Carnegie Steel plant in Homestead, Pittsburgh, Pennsylvania organized themselves and formed a workers' committee. Finally, Henry Frick hired Pinkerton guards to safeguard against interference as he did not trust local law enforcement. The result was that the workers, led by Hugh O'Donnell and the Pinkertons, led by Frederick Hinde would be pitted against each other during a strike and in the end lives would be lost and many others would be injured. In the days after the Homestead Strike incident, Henry Frick survived being shot twice in the neck by anarchist Alexander Berkman. He used the Homestead incident to advance the anarchist movement. John Pierpont Morgan founded his J. Pierpont Morgan

& Company in 1862. In 1871, the Drexel, Morgan & Company was formed as a result of a partnership he made with a Philadelphia firm. In 1879, William Vanderbilt sold his stock in the New York Central Railroad worth eighteen million dollars with help from J. P. Morgan. He brought together George Roberts and Frank Thomas of the Pennsylvania Railroad and himself, and Chauncey Depew of the New York Central Railroad in order to work out an agreement in managing the railroads better. In 1887, the Interstate Commerce Act is approved by the US Congress to end certain inequalities in the railroad industry when providing services to the public. Beginning in December 1888, J. P. Morgan began hosting Madison Avenue summit meetings at his home with the presidents of the major railroad companies to discuss ways to obey the Interstate Commerce Act. In 1893, an economic crisis known as the Panic of 1893 began. The US government continued with the gold standard, in spite of the demand for silver or paper currency. During the Panic of 1893, however, the people preferred gold over paper currency and put a large amount of strain on the US Treasury. In 1895, President Grover Cleveland and Treasury Secretary John Carlisle call upon J. P. Morgan to speak with Assistant Treasury Secretary William Curtis to deal with the financial crisis. J. P. Morgan proposed a confidential contract to be made by President Cleveland and his administration with an investors' syndicate to sell government bonds worth fifty million dollars.

When President Cleveland failed to accept this proposal, J. P. Morgan traveled to Washington, DC, himself to speak to President Cleveland. J. P. Morgan cited the Revised Statutes section 3700 and proposed that President Cleveland get the US Treasury to buy gold coins with bonds, recently issued from a Morgan investors' syndicate. After a bit of skepticism, President Cleveland finally accepted the offer. In 1897, after a meeting with John Gates' attorney Elbert Gary, J. P. Morgan created the Federal Steel Company in 1898. He then purchased Carnegie Steel for $480 million from Andrew Carnegie who retired from the steel industry and went into philanthropy. J. P. Morgan merged Carnegie Steel with Federal Steel and created the United States Steel Company.

Going back to Thomas Edison, Nikola Tesla, and George Westinghouse, I would say that George Westinghouse and Nikola Tesla were the extroverts. They wanted to promote AC electricity because they felt that everyone, urban and rural dwellers, should be able to enjoy the benefits of electricity as a group. Everyone would have to pay their share of the costs for providing this valuable service. A central generating station, owned by a corporation, would produce electricity and distribute it equally to those hooked into a "grid." Thomas Edison, on the other hand, was the introvert. He wanted to promote DC electricity because, not only did he believe that AC electricity was dangerous, but he also felt that large electrical grids would be controlled and owned by ruthless and monopolistic corporations, motivated by profit alone and raising costs at will. This would hurt those who could least afford to pay such high costs. As such, he believed DC electricity would provide the benefits of electricity to small sections of the population. Each section of a city would have its own power plant. The power plants would be under the control of local governments and local laws. A single commissioner would be in charge of each power plant. Thomas Edison was introverted in a sense that he felt his method of providing the public with electricity was the best method and only his method should be accepted. He was also quick to sue others in court with patent infringement. Nikola Tesla was extroverted in a sense that he surrendered all his royalty rights to his employer George Westinghouse in order to make sure there was no trouble in the development of his AC electricity. In regards to the kinetoscope versus the movie projector, the former showing films only to an individual viewer and the latter showing films to a group of viewers at the same time, Thomas Edison was the introvert while his researcher William Kennedy Laurie Dickson was the extrovert.

John D. Rockefeller, Andrew Carnegie, and J. P. Morgan were all extroverted in a sense that they wanted to bring change to their respective industries, as well as being efficient organizers and reorganizers. However, Andrew Carnegie was showing his more introverted side when he hired Henry Frick and let him take charge of his company while he was away in Scotland. Henry Frick's ruthless business practices and his treatment of Carnegie Steel workers show Henry Frick to be Andrew Carnegie's extroverted opposite. John D. Rockefeller and J. P. Morgan were extroverted to a much greater extent than Andrew Carnegie. John D. Rockefeller took charge of the petroleum industry through Standard Oil, reorganized the entire industry, and built up a monopoly through backdoor deals and hostile takeovers of his competitors. J. P. Morgan took charge of the financial and banking industries, brought competing companies together to work out deals, and took charge during the Panic of 1893 in which he saved the US Treasury and brought back the gold standard.

Jacob Riis was a journalist who investigated the slums of New York City. He documented what he saw and published it in his book *How the Other Half Lives: Studies Among the Tenements of New York* in 1890. His book laid the foundation for later journalists who would engage in "muckraking" investigative journalism. Among those journalists were Samuel Sidney McClure who founded *McClure's Magazine* in 1893. Henry Demarest Lloyd published his book *Wealth Against Commonwealth* in 1894 as a criticism against the growing economic power of Standard Oil Company.

Jane Addams founded Hull-House in Chicago in 1889 to assist newly arriving immigrants adapt to a new life in the United States. Jane Addams would set the stage for future social workers and sure enough, it wouldn't be long before Hull-House would get international recognition from such people as Sydney and Beatrice Webb, Keir Hardie, and Aylmer Maude.

Once when Jane Addams caught a burglar who broke into Hull-House one night, she found him a job the next morning instead of having him arrested. Jacob Riis was introverted because he was concerned with getting the facts about the lower-class people who lived in the slums of New York City. He wandered into various neighborhoods, spoke to them, saw their disgusting living conditions, and wanted to expose their miserable status, as a result of unrestrained capitalism, to the middle and upper classes. Jane Addams was the extrovert because she felt as though she could change the lives of others coming to the United States by simply introducing them to

American culture. She was also showing herself as extroverted by seeing "the good" in a Hull-House burglar. Between the late 1830s until World War I, almost all the white community agreed on six "white supremacist propositions," outlined by George Frederickson that characterized racist thought of that time period. Those propositions were: <u>Blacks were different from whites</u>; <u>Black inferiority was the result of that difference</u>; <u>those differences would change very slowly</u>; <u>race mixing between blacks and whites would produce an inferior hybrid</u>; <u>if blacks intrude themselves on whites, strong dislike of the other race would be inevitable</u>; and because of these racist ideas it was believed that, in practical terms, <u>an integrated society was impossible</u>. This racist thought formed the ideology behind the separate but equal Jim Crow segregation laws on passenger trains and other public facilities. The first Jim Crow laws were passed starting with Florida in 1887, Mississippi in 1888, Texas in 1889, and Louisiana in 1890. In 1891, Alabama, Arkansas, Georgia, and Tennessee all passed Jim Crow laws. Another state passed a Jim Crow law in 1892 and the rest would all wait until after the *Plessy v. Ferguson* decision in 1896.

As the Louisiana Separate Car Act was introduced into the state legislature in 1890, African American members of the American Citizens' Equal Rights Association denounced it but it passed both houses of the Louisiana state legislature and was signed into law by Governor Francis T. Nicholls. Newspaper editor Louis Martinet of the New Orleans Crusader was pushing for a "test case" to challenge the Separate Car Law and in 1891, he led a group of African Americans in New Orleans to form the Citizens' Committee to Test the Constitutionality of the Separate Car Law.

Albion Tourgée and James Walker were hired as lawyers. The plan was to have a colored passenger buy an interstate ticket and board a train. The passenger would then refuse to go to the Jim Crow car after being directed there by the conductor, who would then file a complaint under the criminal provision of the Separate Car Law. The next step was finding a suitable client, the first was Daniel Desdunes, but after the charges were dismissed, Albion Tourgée and James Walker had to look for a new client. Homer Plessy bought a ticket on the East Louisiana Railroad and then refused to go to the

Jim Crow car. He violated the Separate Car Law and was arrested. Assistant District Attorney Lionel Adams filed information against Homer Plessy, who was then arraigned by Judge John Ferguson in a Criminal District Court. After being decided in both the Criminal District Court and the Louisiana Supreme Court, it was finally able to be brought in front of the United States Supreme Court.

The former Solicitor General Samuel Philips, who had served on the 1883 Civil Rights Cases, was asked by Albion Tourgée to serve as cocounsel. Albion Tourgée and James Walker submitted a brief starting with an introduction of the case, followed by sections each written by Albion Tourgée and James Walker. The case was presented as follows and was based on "affirmative" national and state citizenship provisions and "restrictive" due process and equal protection provisions. The "restrictive" rights argument was the first argument and emphasized that the Separate Car Law violated both the equal protection and due process provisions of the Fourteenth Amendment Section 1. The "affirmative" rights argument was the second argument and emphasized that the Separate Car Law violated the national and state citizenship provisions of the Fourteenth Amendment Section 1, the Thirteenth Amendment, and the Declaration of Independence. Cocounsel Samuel Philips submitted a brief emphasizing the privileges-or-immunities provision of the Fourteenth Amendment Section 1. His argument was based mostly on that provision and emphasized three statements: Why Albion Tourgée and James Walker failed to establish Homer Plessy's "color" in the *Plessy v. Ferguson* case record; The Separate Car Law allowed for legally enforced inequality; and that American citizens turn to state governments to protect some civil rights and others are protected by the federal government. Interstate (across state lines) travel was protected by the latter. Samuel Philips analyzed the *Washington, Alexandria, and Georgetown Railroad Company v. Brown* case (1873) and an earlier case *Crandall v. Nevada* (1868). These two cases gave official approval to constitutional principles. His conclusion in the end was that it was self-evident and had to be perceived as such in order to be persuasive.

Louisiana Attorney General Milton Cunningham submitted his brief in support of the Separate Car Law and Judge John Ferguson. It focused mostly on the Fourteenth Amendment and used the Civil Rights Case to deny violations of the Thirteenth Amendment. It contained material stating that the law allowed for states to organize people by race using the power of law enforcement officers but could not pass legislation promoting such inequalities. It relied on legal construction of the Separate Car Law by the Louisiana Supreme Court, which didn't exempt railway officials from civil damage liabilities in incorrect assignment cases, equal protection was not denied as a result of the exemption, and the law didn't violate a passenger's life, liberty, or property without due process. Albion Tourgée and James Walker's argument was denied by the state of Louisiana. Milton Cunningham added new material after finding an arbitrary claim insisting that blacks serve on juries. Alexander Morse also submitted a brief that supported the Separate Car Law. It was based on the Slaughterhouse Cases, especially *Barbier v. Connally* (1885) and stated that the states' police power is not made smaller as a result of the Fourteenth Amendment. The United States Supreme Court voted to uphold the Separate Car Law, 7 to 1, on May 18, 1896.

Justice Henry Billings Brown delivered the majority opinion and Justice John Marshall Harlan delivered the dissenting opinion. Louis Martinet, Albion Tourgée, James Walker, and Samuel Philips were all extroverted in a sense that they were willing to risk their careers, Homer Plessy, and even the black community to test the Separate Car Law as unconstitutional. Justice John Marshall Harlan was showing himself as a little extroverted as well when he delivered the opposing opinion. Justice Henry Billings Brown delivered the opinion to uphold the Louisiana Separate Car Law, Jim Crow laws in other states, and racial segregation in general and thus showed himself as introverted.

William Jennings Bryan was born on March 19, 1860. He was born and grew up in Salem, Illinois, the fourth child of Silas and Mariah Bryan. The tradition of evangelical Protestant Christianity he learned from his mother and it influenced his childhood. He attended Baptist, Methodist, and Presbyterian Sunday schools and the McGuffey Reader was an important part of his lessons. He was born into a culture that was based on "political religion" in which the Declaration of Independence and the New Testament were the "twin truths." His parents were strict, loving, and responsible and he was a bit rebellious as a child but he still wanted to please his parents and earn their respect. At age fifteen, he moved to Jacksonville, Illinois to attend Whipple Academy and Illinois College. He came to view Jacksonville as pretty much the same as Salem. His classes centered on Latin and Greek. The school curriculum was more focused on textbook reading and memorizing than on independent critical thinking. He learned from and embraced boosterism, advocating collective goals, strong public spirit, and self-sacrificing citizens. He attended law school in Chicago at the Union School of Law. While he was in Chicago, he viewed it as a city of corruption, poverty, greed, and class warfare and he came to the conclusion that "People were becoming criminally negligent and selfish," as he wrote to Mary Baird, whom he married in 1883 after returning to Jacksonville. At age twenty-seven, he moved to Nebraska with his wife Mary and daughter Ruth and took a job at a law firm in Lincoln.

William Jennings Bryan was a loyal member of the Democratic Party. In college, he read *History of the United States* written by George Bancroft, an Andrew Jackson supporter. He witnessed the 1876 Democratic Party convention in St. Louis, Missouri. In the 1880s, politics in Nebraska consisted of where colleges, prisons, state hospitals, etc. were to be located and provide local jobs. Politics at federal level consisted of providing economic aid through tariff protection and land grants and the major political parties believed that the federal government's main job was growth promotion and productivity in the economy. Progress and prosperity were the agendas that everyone from politicians to the constituents themselves stood united toward. However, in the 1880s, the interests of the individual local government were placed ahead of the collective interests of the nation as a whole. William Jennings Bryan set out to establish friendships with major Nebraska power figures, such as J. Sterling Morton in 1888. He gave a speech on tariff reform at the 1888 Democratic Party convention nominating President Grover Cleveland for reelection. In 1890, he was elected to the United States House of Representatives and served as representative for Nebraska's First Congressional District. The Populist Movement began to take form among farmers within the same year. Among the political reforms advocated by Populists were initiative and referendum, secret ballot, and the direct election of United States Senators, rather than chosen by state legislatures. Economic reforms advocated by Populists were to bring transportation, banking, and communication centers to the control of the federal government. Cultural reforms advocated by Populists were that the laborers could enjoy the goods they made. The Populists were strongest in the South, West, and Great Plains and in most of these states they were on third-party tickets. The Populist party took control of the Nebraska state legislature and local offices. William Jennings Bryan shared a vision with the Populists that the producers of goods could supply the community and advance their profits at the same time.

On March 16, 1892, he made his first address to the United States House of Representatives. It was a three-hour long speech speaking out against protective high tariffs and legislation that favored a select few on top but overlooked and hurt ordinary farmers and workers. William Jennings Bryan was reelected in the 1892 elections with help from Populists James Weaver and Mary Lease. The Democratic Party of Nebraska was falling apart for several reasons. President Grover Cleveland had just appointed J. Sterling Morton as secretary of agriculture, ignoring party reformers in the process. J. Sterling Morton turned away from his alliance with William Jennings Bryan and began speaking against the Populists and the Populist Movement. President Cleveland began to look upon some of his fellow Democrats as his enemies in order to get the mints to stop their quest for silver. On August 16, 1893, William Jennings Bryan made a speech advocating bimetallism in which silver and gold would be used together to back the money supply. In 1894, he made the decision not to run for reelection to keep his seat in the United States House of Representatives but instead chose to run for a seat in the United States Senate unsuccessfully.

On July 9, 1896, he delivered his "Cross of Gold" speech at the Democratic National Convention in Chicago. He won the democratic presidential nomination the next day with Arthur Sewall as the vice presidential candidate. Arthur Sewall was a silver-backer and businessman from Maine and was chosen because he could help persuade Northeastern voters to vote for William Jennings Bryan and the Democratic Party. The money issue was central to the 1896 Bryan/Sewall presidential campaign. He received support from Populist leaders, S. F. Norton and John Peter Altgeld from Illinois, Willa Cather, and Ignatius Donnelly. Ohio Governor William McKinley won the Republican presidential nomination with Garret Hobart as the vice presidential candidate. Mark Hanna was the main political advisor and campaign manager of the McKinley/Hobart presidential campaign, as well as Governor McKinley's friend.

William Jennings Bryan campaigned by going to his supporters by traveling around the country by train. Governor McKinley campaigned on the front porch of his house in Canton, Ohio where his supporters came to him and he gave speeches that were popular even among farmers and workers, as well as linking <u>nationalism</u>, <u>stability</u>, <u>law and order</u>, and <u>business prosperity</u> to the Republican Party. Governor McKinley's campaign received funding from a variety of major corporations, industrialists, and bankers including J. P. Morgan, John D. Rockefeller, and Andrew Carnegie. This funding exceeded that of William Jennings Bryan, his campaign, and the Democratic Party. On Election Day November 3, 1896, William Jennings Bryan received 6,509,052 votes. He won twenty-two states, all the Southern states and most of the Western states.

However, William Jennings Bryan lost the election to Governor McKinley, with two likely factors contributing: that William Jennings Bryan failed to get voters in the Midwestern states of Minnesota, Michigan, Illinois, Indiana, and Wisconsin and that William Jennings Bryan was unable to get very many urban voters. Governor McKinley, on the other hand, was able to attract young men and immigrant voters within the Midwestern states. William Jennings Bryan published *The First Battle: A Story of the Campaign of 1896* as an account of the presidential election of 1896.

Four years later, as the 1900 presidential election approaches, William Jennings Bryan begins his second race for the presidency after accepting the Democratic presidential nomination in Indianapolis, Indiana. President McKinley accepted the Republican presidential nomination with New York Governor Theodore Roosevelt as the vice presidential candidate. Two months later, William Jennings Bryan gave a speech at the Democratic National Convention in Kansas City, Missouri, detailing how when the United States won the Spanish-American War in 1899 and captured Cuba, the Philippines, Guam, and Puerto Rico as territories shows imperialism. He stated his opposition to imperialism in the speech before taking Adlai E. Stevenson as the vice presidential candidate. Mark Hanna, who was elected US Senator from Ohio in 1897, was once again the campaign manager for the McKinley/Roosevelt presidential campaign. William Jennings Bryan gave 546 speeches throughout the campaign while Theodore Roosevelt, campaigning for President McKinley, gave 673 speeches throughout the campaign. Once again the Republicans had more money at their disposal than the Democrats. William Jennings Bryan ended up losing once again to incumbent President McKinley and Vice President Theodore Roosevelt.

William Jennings Bryan begins his third and final presidential campaign in 1908 by having his brother Charles Bryan ask Progressive Democrats to form Bryan Clubs. President Theodore Roosevelt chooses William Howard Taft to be the Republican presidential nominee, with James Sherman as the vice presidential candidate, rather than running himself. William Jennings Bryan gave his acceptance speech in Lincoln, Nebraska in August 12, 1908. In the speech, "Shall the People Rule" was the question he asked constantly and he proposed two options: all campaign donations over one hundred dollars would have to be made public prior to an election, and no more than ten thousand dollars can be contributed by anyone. His third proposal was the direct election of United States Senators. On August 25, 1908, he gave another speech in Indianapolis, Indiana, in which he proposed a plan that business corporations must apply for a federal license if they control more than 25 percent of a product and could not have more than 50 percent control. He also supported anti-trust legislation in the speech. On August 27, 1908, he gave another speech in Topeka, Kansas, where he proposed taxing the banks in order to protect the people's deposits. He allied himself with American Federation of Labor (AFL) President Samuel Gompers and the Labor Movement. William Jennings Bryan took John Kern as his vice presidential candidate and won all the Southern states but beyond that he only won Kentucky, Oklahoma, Nebraska, Colorado, and Nevada. Despite his hard work, the Republican opposition defeated him once again through William Howard Taft and James Sherman. He may have lost the presidential election, but on the other hand, he helped the Democratic Party win eight seats in the United States House of Representatives, governorships in Ohio, Indiana, Minnesota, Nebraska, etc. as well as the Nebraska state legislature.

William Jennings Bryan was very much extroverted. He played a very central role in politics during the 1890s and into the early twentieth century. He was at the center of the Progressive movement from the 1900s to 1925. He set up his own newspaper *The Commoner* in order to spread his political views to the general public. He ran for president of the United States three times on the Democratic Party ticket, despite being defeated each time by the Republican opposition. In 1912, he was rewarded with the position of secretary of state by Woodrow Wilson for his service with the Wilson campaign. In 1925, before his death, he stood in opposition to evolution during the Scopes "Monkey" Trial. William Jennings Bryan supported the Populist Movement, free silver, and Prohibition, challenging the traditional Democratic Party establishment in the process. He also supported the Christian fundamentalists by participating in the Scopes Trial. Republican Presidents William McKinley and William Howard Taft were exactly the opposite. They were very much introverted because they were elected with the support of those who favored the establishment. They wanted a more secure and stable United States and felt that that could only be maintained with support from the traditional "big business" industrialists (Rockefeller, Carnegie, and Morgan).

The politics of the Spanish-American War begin with the Cuban Insurrection in 1892 that was led by José Martí, Tomás Estrada Palma, Máximo Gómez, Antonio Maceo, Serafin Sanchez, and Carlos Roloff, along with two thousand other Cuban who were members of the Cuban Revolutionary Party. On March 23, 1895, José Martí and Máximo Gómez laid out the principles of the revolution in a manifesto stating that Cuban blacks were to participate, noncombatants could not be attacked and rural wealth could not be destroyed. Between March 31, and April 11, 1895, as the insurrection began and José Martí was killed in an ambush in Dos Rios. Máximo Gómez' policy was to cause an economic depression in Cuba by attacking its main export industry, sugar, and force Spanish-supporting Cubans to back the revolution. Spain would not be able to afford to keep control of Cuba and would grant Cubans independence. Antonio Maceo's policy was to force sugar planters to cooperate with the revolutionary agenda by threatening to destroy their crops if they refused. Eventually, Máximo Gómez' policy would have greater influence in the revolution over the latter's policy. Two months later, on July 15, 1895, the Republic of Cuba became independent and a provisional government was established a month later. Spanish Prime Minister Antonio Cánovas del Castillo came to power on March 14, 1895, and decided to put a stop to the Cuban Insurrection by sending General Arsenio Martinez de Campos to Cuba. General Martinez de Campos' plan was to keep the revolutionaries confined to the far eastern side of Cuba in the Oriente Province, man a two-hundred-yard wide and fifty-mile long defense line from Morón to Júcaro, and send out the ship *Reina Mercedes* to Cuba with 850 troops on board. After this plan failed, Prime Minister Antonio Cánovas del Castillo replaced General Martinez de Campos with General Valeriano Weyler y Nicolau on February 10, 1896. General Weyler y Nicolau pursued a policy of reconcentration where military leaders acted against the revolutionaries and anyone aiding a revolutionary faced the wrath of military law. Nobody could travel without permission and anyone living around Sancti Spíritus, Puerto Principe, and Santiago de Cuba had to relocate near military headquarters. General Weyler y Nicolau's military strategy was based on a defense line from Morón to Júcaro, keeping Oriente and Camagüey and a defense line remote from Mariel and Majana, separating Pinar del Río in the West from the east. The center provinces of Havana, Matanzas, and Santa Clara were directly in the middle of those two defense lines. General Weyler y Nicolau's plan was to begin in Pinar del Río against Antonio Maceo, then focus on Havana and Matanza, and finally anyone who continued to resist would be pushed forward toward the defense line Morón and Júcaro.

However, the defense line plan failed and the revolutionaries ended up winning. On June 12, 1895, President Grover Cleveland and his secretary of state, Richard Olney, issued a neutrality proclamation that broke international law by refusing to give rights to the Cuban revolutionaries. Neither President Cleveland, nor his Secretary of State Olney had very much sympathy for the Cuban revolutionaries and were mainly concerned only with preventing a war from happening. On April 6, 1896, President Cleveland and the executive branch were called upon by both houses of congress to recognize the Cuban revolutionaries through a joint resolution. As President Grover Cleveland neared the end of his term, he continued refusing to recognize the Cuban revolutionaries and their government as he stated in a speech he gave on December 7, 1896, President Cleveland's proposals were pushing for Cuban home rule with no success. On October 8, 1897, the battleship Maine was sent to Port Royal, South Carolina, and then two months later it was sent to Key West, Florida. Consul General Fitzhugh Lee in Havana wanted two navy ships waiting at Key West to be sent off to Havana if necessary and for extra security measures; other ships should go to Dry Torugas. Commanding officers of Cuban home guards opposed to the revolutionaries got angry at newspapers in Havana criticizing General Weyler y Nicolau and ordered a riot. Consul General Fitzhugh Lee was at first thinking about sending the Maine but settled toward keeping things under control after the riot ended. However, President William McKinley thought otherwise and on January 24, 1898, he decided to send the Maine anyway. Consul General Fitzhugh Lee persisted by pushing to delay sending the Maine for a couple of days while tensions die down some more.

But President McKinley once again ignored the Consul General's advice. Finally, Consul General Lee stated that the Cuban autonomy policy would be weakened if the Maine was brought into Havana. The Maine was sent toward Havana and anchored in the harbor the next day on January 25, 1898. Charles D. Sigsbee, the captain, made official visits and attended events without difficulty. On February 1, 1898, he suggested a more powerful battleship such as the Texas, the Massachusetts, or the Iowa act as a relief vessel to the Maine. When Secretary of the Navy John D. Long wanted to remove the Maine from the Havana harbor for sanitary reasons, Consul General Lee objected. On February 9, 1898, Spanish Minister Enrique Dupuy de Lôme published a letter in the New York Journal. It referred to President McKinley in a very negative way. Enrique Dupuy de Lôme resigned as Spanish minister the next day on February 10, 1898, as a result of his comments and the day after that Juan du Bosc became the new Spanish minister. On February 15, 1898, the Maine exploded in the Havana harbor which made Cuba a central issue in politics.

American Commodore George Dewey entered Manila Bay with only six ships—the *Olympia*, the *Baltimore*, the *Raleigh*, the *Boston*, the *Concord*, and the *Petrel*. None of which were armored. The first four were well-protected cruisers with large and powerful guns. The latter two were unprotected and good for very little. Commodore Dewey had only 1,611 crew members for each of his ships. On the opposite side, Spanish Admiral Patricio Montojo entered Cañacao Bay with seven ships, the Reina Cristina, the Castilla, the Don Juan de Austria, the Don Antonio de Ulloa, the Isla de Cuba, the Marques del Duero, and the Isla de Luzon. Of the seven Spanish ships, two were unprotected, one was made of wood, and the other four were gunboats. On May 1, 1898, at 5:05 a.m., the Battle of Manila Bay began when the Spanish opened fire. The Boston and the Concord responded by firing back. At 5:15 a.m., the Spanish again opened fired on the Americans. At 5:40 a.m., Commodore Dewey turned to his commander, who then ordered the Olympia to fire an eight-inch shell, signaling the other ships to begin firing. At 7:00 a.m., Spanish Admiral Montojo commanded the Reina Cristina to attack the Olympia. This turned out to be a mistake since the Reina Cristina was much slower than the Olympia and was vulnerable to attack by the whole American naval unit. Spanish Admiral Montojo decided to make the Isla de Cuba the lead ship of his naval unit. At 7:30 a.m., Captain Gridley reported that the Olympia was running low on ammunition. At 8:00 a.m., Admiral Montojo commanded some of his ships near to Bacoor Bay and away from Canacao Bay. At 11:16 a.m., the Battle of Manila Bay came to a conclusion, a white flag was raised an hour later and at 12:30 p.m., the Battle of Manila Bay ended. After all had fighting ceased, Commodore Dewey sent out the Petrel to finish off remaining Spanish ships in Cavite harbor. Its lieutenant, Edward Hughes, and seven sailors, set a number of these ships on fire. The Spanish suffered severe casualties up to 371. The Americans only suffered minor damage and no deaths.

On April 26, 1898, one month before the Battle in Manila Bay, President William McKinley issued a declaration respecting the 1856 Paris Declaration. The Americans were beginning a blockade of Cuba and on April 27, Admiral Sampson stationed the New York, Puritan, and Amphitrite at Matanzas. Spanish Admiral Pascual Cervera left for San Juan, Puerto Rico on April 29 with four armored cruisers and three torpedo-boat destroyers. These ships were the *Infanta Maria Teresa*, the *Vizcaya*, the *Cristobal Colon*, the *Almirante Oquendo*, the *Pluton*, the *Furor*, and the *Terror*. The four armored cruisers were captained by Victor Concas, Antonio Eulate, Emilio Moreau, and Joaquin Lazaga. The three torpedo-boat destroyers were captained by Fernando Villaamil. The American Navy sent out the Harvard and the St. Louis, captained by Charles Cotton and Casper Goodrich, to obstruct Admiral Cervera in the Windward Islands' east waters. The Yale was sent to Puerto Rico two days later. On May 10, Captain Villaamil called for information on Admiral Sampson's Movements and fuel supplies while at Fort de France. Meanwhile, the Harvard completed its patrol of Martinique's east side. On May 12, Captain Villaamil had to report to Admiral Cervera that he was refused coal in Martinique. Also, the Yale had arrived in San Juan, Puerto Rico and Cuba was blockaded. The American naval unit attacked San Juan at 5:10 a.m. On May 14, Admiral Cervera went to the Dutch island of Curacao where the governor only allowed him six hundred tons of coal for two of his ships, the Vizcaya and the Infanta Maria Teresa. On May 19, at 9:00 a.m., Admiral Cervera arrived at Santiago de Cuba. Afterward, Admiral Sampson moved toward Cap-Haïtien, Haiti, and arrived there on May 18 at 4:00 p.m. Earlier the same day, Commodore Winfield Schley joins Admiral Sampson in Key West, Florida, at 1:00 a.m. They have a meeting and arrange for the flying squadron to move to Cienfuegos. On May 19, it was reported that the Spanish naval unit had arrived in Santiago de Cuba harbor. The St. Paul, the Harvard, and the St. Louis were all patrolling the Caribbean Sea, along with the Minneapolis, but only the St. Paul and the Harvard received the message. On May 21, both the Yale and the St. Paul arrived in Santiago de Cuba, with the Harvard and Minneapolis following on May 23. On May 26, Commodore Schley came and went near Santiago de Cuba. From 7:30 p.m. to 1:00 p.m. the next day, he stopped the naval unit and drifted. On May 28, Commodore Schley was ordered to stay in Santiago de Cuba. At 2:00 p.m. on May 31, with the Iowa, the Massachusetts, and the New Orleans, he fired at the Spanish Cristobal Colon, which returned fire until 3:00 p.m. On June 1, Admiral Sampson arrived at the Santiago de Cuba blockade at 6:30 a.m. with his forces that included the Oregon, the New York, and the Porter. They joined Commodore Schley and the flying squadron there. Spanish Admiral Cervera was now blockaded in port with his forces. Naval Constructor Richmond Hobson was given the honor of sinking the Merrimac by Admiral Sampson. On June 2, Admiral Sampson divided his ships into two groups, one commanded by himself, and the other commanded by Commodore Schley. The result was an arc around Morro castle. At 3:00 a.m., on June 3, everything started out okay until the Spanish opened fired. Six underwater mines at Estrella Point and two at Socapa Point exploded. Hobson and his crew got away unharmed but failed to sink the Merrimac. From 7:30 a.m. to 10:30 a.m., on June 6, Admiral Sampson ordered the Texas, the Massachusetts, the Iowa, and the Oregon to fire at Spanish batteries. Nine Spanish defenders were killed and Don Emilio-Acosta, second-in-command of the *Reina Mercedes*, was wounded. On June 7, Admiral Sampson changed his nighttime plans to three picket launches a mile from Morro. Two miles out farther, the Vixen, the Suwannee, and the Dolphin had to line up. Four miles out farther, the rest of the ships in an arc. On June 8, the Iowa, the Oregon, and the Massachusetts were ordered to each take two hours going up the channel every night using their searchlights. The Brooklyn, the Texas, the New York, and the New Orleans were ordered to do the same. On June 9, Commander Bowman H. McCalla and the Marblehead arrived at Guantanamo. Lieutenant-Colonel Robert Huntington and the First Marine Battalion arrived at Guantanamo Bay on June 10. The next day, a combat began lasting for three days. By June 15, Spanish troops had been cleared from the area and six American lives were lost.

In 1898, the War Department was in charge of the United States Army and was headed by two Civil War veterans. Russell Alger, Michigan politician and businessman, was Secretary of War and Major-General Nelson Miles from Massachusetts was the US Army's commanding general and the War Department's lead military officer. The War Department consisted of ten bureaus, each headed by a Brigadier General. The job of the Secretary of War was to work with the Department's bureaus in order to organize and carry out the US Army's financial matters.

The job of the commanding general was to transmit orders from the president and the secretary of war to the bureaus. The commanding general only had direct control over the departments of the Adjutant and Inspector Generals, fighting units, and staff officers trained for field service.

On March 9, 1898, the Fifty Million Dollar Bill was passed by the US Congress and the US Navy took advantage of it right away and bought more ships and hired more personnel. The War Department spent ten million dollars and $5.5 million on coastal defenses. On March 17, Republican US Representative John Hull introduced his "Hull Bill" on behalf of the War Department that called for expanding the army to 104,000 troops. It was opposed by southern Democrats who supported the state militias and believed that it would eventually reduce state volunteers' role in the federal military. On April 7, they formed a coalition referring the Hull Bill to a committee and never passed in the US Congress. On April 9, General Miles's plan was an expeditionary force of one hundred thousand troops, fifty thousand state volunteers, sixty-two thousand troops for the regular army, fifty thousand militia auxiliary troops, and etc. On April 15, twenty-two infantry regiments were sent to ports in New Orleans, Mobile, and Tampa. Artillery units and six cavalry regiments were sent to Camp Thomas, Tennessee. The former three were commanded by brigadier generals: William Shafter, John Coppinger, and James Wade. The latter was commanded by a Major-General John Brooke. On April 20, President McKinley came to the conclusion that the US Army was unable to enter the battlefield at a White House war council. On April 22, he called for 125,000 volunteers. Four days later, the US Congress passed a bill that expanded the regular army. In the new law, 64,719 soldiers became the army's strength. Also included in the law was the size of combat branch units: 106 soldiers for an infantry unit, one hundred soldiers for a cavalry troop, two hundred soldiers for a heavy artillery battery, 173 soldiers for a light artillery battery, and 150 soldiers for an engineer unit and soldiers would receive a 20 percent increase in their pay. On May 25, President McKinley called for more volunteers of seventy-five thousand. The United States Volunteers supplied the soldiers or both volunteer calls. Most Americans were enthusiastic about the United States entering the war so getting citizens to join the army wasn't much of a problem. William Cody (Buffalo Bill), Frank James (Jessie James's brother), the New York Journal, Martha Shute, etc. were among those who made strange proposals to the War Department. Company K, First Connecticut had volunteers ranging in age from twenty-three to twenty-four and consisted of salesmen, students, industrial workers, electricians, etc. The 161st Indiana average age was twenty-six and consisted of farmers, merchants, professionals, skilled and common workers, and clerks. Up to ten thousand blacks entered the four regiments of the United States Infantry Volunteers: Seventh, Eighth, Ninth, and Tenth. Training camps for volunteer units were set up in Tennessee, Virginia, California, and Florida. Because of overcrowding and unclean conditions, by September 30, 425 soldiers were at Camp Thomas, 246 were at Jacksonville, 107 were at Camp Alger, and 139 were at San Francisco. Toward the end of President

McKinley's administration, the anarchist movement began to reach its height in which his assassin, Leon Czolgosz, would take center stage by shooting and killing President McKinley himself. As I discuss Leon Czolgosz, I will also bring up his political influences, and talk a little about President McKinley himself.

Leon Czolgosz was the fourth child of Polish immigrants and was baptized into the Catholic Church and raised in Detroit, Michigan. His family moved around all the time during his childhood. At ten years old, he was smart and obedient and would allow himself to be punished. In 1883, his mother died after giving birth to a tenth child named Victoria. He was hired as a factory worker at the Cleveland Rolling Mill Company at age seventeen and quickly proved to be a good worker, but after the 1893 financial crisis, he lost his job but was rehired as "Fred Nieman" under a new boss. He eventually lost faith and interest in the Catholic church he was brought up in and he began to read Edward Bellamy's *Looking Backward: 2000–1887* which gave him a lot of influence. He joined the Golden Eagle Society and met Anton Zuolinski of the Sila, an educational club. Leon Czolgosz joined Sila and became interested in anarchism. He contracted syphilis, quit his job, and moved onto his family's farm where he refused to do much work other than make a few repairs. He mostly just laid around, played with the children, hunted rabbits, or went fishing in a pond. The only time he actually applied for a job was as a conductor for the Stanley Company.

When Italian immigrant Gaetano Bresci of Paterson, New Jersey, assassinated Italian King Umberto I on July 29, 1900, Leon Czolgosz read about the assassination and then saved the article and put it in his wallet. He began to despise his stepmother, Catarina, and couldn't stand to be in the same room as her. He went to Canton, Ohio, to see President McKinley give a speech at his house during the 1900 presidential election. On May 5, 1901, he attended Emma Goldman's "Modern Phases of Anarchy" lecture at Cleveland's Memorial Hall and suddenly became inspired to become a radical social revolutionary. That same night, he purchased a radical newspaper called *Free Society*. On May 19, 1901, Leon Czolgosz met with Emil Schilling, who invited him to dinner and gave him a book that he later returned during his second visit when he was told to go to Chicago to meet Emma Goldman. On July 11, 1901, he finally left his family's farm. His family got sick of having him around and gave him seventy dollars to leave.

On July 12, 1901, Emma Goldman and Mary were about to leave *Free Society* publisher Abraham Isaak's house when Leon Czolgosz arrived at the door, presenting himself as "Fred Nieman." Emma Goldman and Leon Czolgosz talked together while on a train riding through Chicago. At Lake Shore Station, Leon Czolgosz was introduced to Emma Goldman's friends, including Hippolyte Havel, a Czechoslovakian radical. Leon Czolgosz began chatting about anarchism with Abraham Isaak, who in turn, was becoming very suspicious of Leon Czolgosz and wrote a letter to Emil Schilling. On September 1, 1901, Abraham Isaak published a warning about Leon Czolgosz being a government spy in the Free Society. Emma Goldman became angry over the article that falsely accused Leon Czolgosz of being a spy and forced those responsible to make a public apology. Leon Czolgosz went to Buffalo, New York in the summer of 1901, ether because of its Polish population or the Pan-American Exposition. He made friends with two Polish workers, among them Antoine Kazmerek who offered him a bed in his four room house for a month fee of three dollars, including washing/laundry. Just like on the family farm, he still kept mostly to himself but he was now taking care of himself more and keeping his appearance up. When he decided to leave the Kazmareks for Cleveland, instead of paying his room fee, he offered his revolver instead. He bought anarchist material in Cleveland, then went to Chicago and saw an article about President McKinley soon to be arriving in Buffalo for the an-American Exposition. He immediately bought a train ticket back to Buffalo. On September 4, 1901, President McKinley arrived at the Exposition with his wife Ida, Dr. Rixey, SS *George Foster*, Samuel Ireland, Albert Gallagher, and others. Leon Czolgosz bought a .32 caliber Johnson revolver from Walbridge's Hardware Store. He would not be able to carry out the assassination until the 6th.

On September 6, 1901, both Leon Czolgosz and President McKinley woke up early in the morning. President McKinley visited

Niagara Falls and Leon Czolgosz followed him there but failed at an assassination attempt and went back to the Exposition in Buffalo. At 4:00 p.m., President McKinley was greeting people at the Temple of Music and Leon Czolgosz would have to wait his turn in a slow-moving, long line, with police and soldiers watching. Leon Czolgosz held his gun under a white handkerchief and fired the first shot and then fired a second shot, both at President McKinley's chest. President McKinley then clutched his chest with a confused expression on his face. Before Leon Czolgosz could take another shot, African American James Parker struck him in the neck with one hand and used his other hand to grab for the revolver.

Francis O'Brien, Detective John Geary, George Foster, Albert Gallagher, and others all swung their fists at Leon Czolgosz who said "I done my duty" as he was being dragged down. John Geary, George Cortelyou, and John Milburn dragged President McKinley over to a chair where he exposed his wounds and called on his present friends to stop beating on Leon Czolgosz who was taken to a small corner room of the Temple of Music. President McKinley was carried off in an electric-powered ambulance and taken to the fair hospital while Leon Czolgosz was taken to the police station where he made a confession:

> I am an Anarchist. I am a disciple of Emma Goldman. Her words set me on fire. I don't regret my act, because I was doing what I could for the great cause.

The next day, on September 7, 1901, he stated the following:

> I don't believe in the Republican form of government, and I don't believe we should have any rulers. It is right to kill them. I don't believe in voting, it is against my principles. I am an Anarchist. I don't believe in marriage. I believe in free love. I fully understood what I was doing when I shot the President. I realized that I was sacrificing my life. I am willing to take the consequences. I know what will happen to me, if the President dies I will be hung. I want to say to

be published—I killed President McKinley because I done my duty. I don't believe in one man having so much service and another man should have none.

His brother Jacob, his stepmother Catarina, and even his own father Paul had nothing to say in Leon's own defense. They all despised him for his laziness and hoped the criminal justice system would do its job and punish him. When President McKinley arrived at the Exposition hospital, the best surgeon in Buffalo, Dr. Roswell Park was in Niagara Falls so Danish immigrant Dr. Herman Mynter and Dr. Matthew Mann were brought in instead. According to Dr. Mann, one bullet did not succeed in forcing a way deep into President McKinley's body and fell out when he was being undressed. The other bullet sliced into the left side of his abdomen. Dr. Matthew Mann eventually decided to leave the bullet where it was and close the wound with black silk. Dr. Rixey did not inform Ida of the shooting until after the surgery was finished and she waited until President McKinley's ambulance to arrive. On September 10, 1901, Emma Goldman was placed under arrest in Chicago at Mr. and Mrs. Norris' apartment and brought to Harrison Street Police Station. Quoting from Alice Wexler's "Emma Goldman: An Intimate Life," she was wearing a white shirtwaist, dark blue cheviot skirt, patent leather boots, and a straw hat with a dotted veil. She was surrounded by reporters as she was being interrogated and made this statement: "Leon Czolgosz, I am convinced, planned the deed unaided and entirely alone. There is no Anarchist ring which would help him. There may be Anarchists who would murder, but there are also men in every walk of life who sometimes feel the impulse to kill. I do not know surely, but I think Czolgosz was one of those downtrodden men who see all the misery which the rich inflict upon the poor, who think of it, who brood over it, and then, in despair, resolve to strike a great blow, as they think, for the good of their fellow-men. But that is not Anarchy. Czolgosz, may have been inspired by me, but if he was, he took the wrong way of showing it."

On September 13, 1901, President McKinley was now in critical condition. Gangrene developed on his stomach walls, poisoning his blood. Newspapers published the events of McKinley's condition for the general public. Cabinet members, friends, and family members visited him for the last time. His wife Ida sat in a chair next to him, and once sung, "Nearer, My God, to Thee." He drifted in and out of consciousness periodically. At 2:15 a.m., on September 14, 1901, President McKinley died.

On September 23, 1901, Leon Czolgosz was led down a dark tunnel from Erie County Penitentiary to the New York Supreme Court. His lawyers, Loran Lewis and Robert Titus, never worked as trial lawyers and were very unenthusiastic about defending an anarchist. Much of his trial focused on the medical attention given to President McKinley and the mentality of Leon Czolgosz himself. He refused to cooperate with his lawyers and the two psychologists who evaluated him, Dr. Carlos MacDonald and Dr. Arthur Hurd. The jury reached the verdict after 33 minutes in the deliberation room. He was found guilty of first degree murder. Thursday, September 26, 1901, at 2:00 p.m., was his sentencing date. Among those who came to visit himwere his brother and sister, Waldek and Victoria, and his father, Paul, who only shook his hand. When they left, Victoria kissed him goodbye while Paul and Waldek held his hand. He was sentenced to death for the week of October 28, 1901. He had a large meal before leaving Buffalo. He was brought to Auburn Prison by train and then he was escorted by police through an angry mob of people to a prison guard named John Martin, who grabbed him, tossed him through the gates, and dragged him on his stomach and knees down the hall, screaming "Save Me! Save Me!" His cell was well guarded to prevent the other prisoners from trying to kill him.

Fellow death row prisoners, Clarence Egnor and Fred Krist both mocked and insulted him while two Catholic priests, Reverend T. Szandinski and Reverend Hyacinth Fudzinski were unsuccessful trying to convert him away from anarchy. On October 29, 1901, he got dressed in a dark gray shirt, a pair of shoes, and dark pants with a slit on the left side and was carried to the electric chair. His final words: "I killed the President for the good of the laboring people, the good people. I am not sorry for my crime but I am sorry I can't see my father."

Warden Mead ordered him to be executed by 1,700 volts through his body, with full current on for forty-five seconds. The electrician slowly through the switch back until the current cut off. Leon Czolgosz was mostly introverted in childhood and into early adulthood. He had very little sympathy for others, he kept to himself in public, and concealed his identity with "Fred Nieman." After the 1893 crisis, he started to become more extroverted. He joined clubs and began hanging out with radicals. This is when he became introduced to the anarchist philosophy. After the assassination of Italian King Umberto I, he became more drawn to anarchism and began sympathizing with lawbreaking anarchists including the assassin Gaetano Bresci and Emma Goldman. When he finally carried out the assassination of President McKinley, he believed he was doing the "right thing" for people and felt no remorse for his act.

With the exception of John D. Rockefeller and Andrew Carnegie, the nineteenth-century upper class was very individualistic and very introverted. The nineteenth-century working class and farmers were extroverted in a sense that they were group-centered, supported mutualism and trade unions, and expected their children to contribute to the family income. However, as the life stories of Rahel Golub and Hamlin Garland illustrate, even workers and farmers were a bit individualistic. The nineteenth-century middle class was originally very introverted. They held values that were very individual-centered such as domesticity, hard work, self-restraint, and individualism. They limited the number of children they produced and expected them to go to school to prepare for their white-collar careers. They lived in Victorian-style houses that consisted of such styles as Queen Anne, Gothic Revival, Colonial Revival, Shingle Style, and Romanesque and located in suburbs away from the wealthy and working classes. These houses included separate bedrooms upstairs for both parents and children, parlor, sitting room, bathroom, etc. The life story of Charles and Mary Acheson Spencer and their seven children who lived on Amberson Avenue in Shadyside, Pittsburgh, Pennsylvania are an example of the nineteenth-century middle-class lifestyle. Eventually the nineteenth-century middle class started to become more extroverted as progressivism began to emerge from within their ranks.

In 1888, Edward Bellamy published *Looking Backward 2000–1887*. It gave people a view of life in the year 2000 from the perspective of the nineteenth century. In the late nineteenth century, women's colleges were being founded. These included Smith College, Wellesley College, Bryn Mawr College, Pennsylvania College for Women, etc. Male colleges and universities began accepting female applicants. The middle-class peace treaty between men and women began with the <u>elimination of the double standard of male behavior</u>. This included allowing women to have control of their bodies, men should have more regard for women's needs, household chores, being fathers, and should refrain from alcohol, pornography, prostitution, and gambling. The next step was <u>easing women's domestic burdens</u> which included replacing the Victorian house with apartments and the use of public kitchens and childcare. The last step was to <u>increase women's public opportunities</u> which included informal education, the right to vote, and work outside the home. The middle-class peace treaty was promoted by the Physicians' Club of Chicago through the "Sexual Hygiene" pamphlet, Marion Talbot and Ellen Swallow Richards through the home economics movement, the National Federation of Women's Clubs, the Chautauqua Movement's Literary and Scientific Circle, and the National American Woman Suffrage Association (NAWSA). With the support of Susan B. Anthony, Elizabeth Cady Stanton, Carrie Chapman Catt, and NAWSA, Wyoming became the first state to grant voting rights to women in 1890, followed by Colorado in 1893, and Utah in 1896. Lizzie Shannon applied for a federal clerkship in 1893. In the 1900 US Census, 5.1 million white-collar workers, male and female, 14 and over were counted.

During the Progressive Era (1901–1921), the presidents were Theodore Roosevelt (1901–1909), William Howard Taft (1909–1913), and Woodrow Wilson (1913–1921). During the Roosevelt administration, alcohol, prostitution, and divorce were the three major social problems in the United States. By 1900, only Kansas, Maine, and North Dakota had statewide prohibition laws. The average consumption of beer and liquor reached 1.2 billion gallons, and the number of saloons reached to 250,000. Major prohibition organizations were the Prohibition Party, the Women's Christian Temperance Union (WCTU), the Anti-Saloon League, and the working-class Protestant Swedes of Worchester, Massachusetts. The "social evil" of prostitution existed in urban "red light" districts such as Manhattan's The Tenderloin, Washington, DC's Hooker's Division, Memphis's Gayosa Street, Chicago's The Levee, New Orleans' Storyville, San Francisco's The Barbary Coast, etc. Major anti-prostitution organization were American Purity Alliance, Society for the Prevention of Crime, American Society of Sanitary and Moral Prophylaxis, NYC's Committee of Fifteen and Committee of Fourteen. In 1902, the Committee of Fifteen published, *The Social Evil.* Divorce mills were places out west where it was quick and easy to get a divorce, as long as the divorcing couple followed residency requirements, including Sioux Falls, South Dakota, Fargo, North Dakota, Guthrie, Oklahoma, etc. In 1900, the national divorce rate was up to 4.0 due in part to middle-class couples breaking up. In 1906, when the National Conference on Uniform Divorce Law met in Washington, DC, only Delaware, New Jersey, and Wisconsin agreed to its recommendations. In 1909, South Dakota's new one-year residency requirement for divorcing couples went into effect. By 1910, the national divorce rate was up to 4.5.

With the use of settlement houses, Young Men's Christian Association (YMCA), theSalvation Army, and the Institutional Church League, the progressives were able to get working class support for New York's Tenement House Commission in 1900, Chicago City Homes Association in 1900, New York's Committee on Congestion of Population in 1907, and Washington, DC's National Association for City Planning in 1909. Through the Country Life Movement, the progressives were able to get the support of farmers for the Country Life Commission in 1908. The first juvenile court was established in Chicago in 1899, the Southern Education Board in 1901, the Public Schools Athletic League in 1903, the National Child Labor Committee in 1904, the Federated Boys' Club in 1906, the Playground Association of America in 1906, and the White

House Conference on the Care of Dependent Children in 1909, all were established to teach working-class children the values of the middle class.

During the Civil War, there were the Molly Maguires and the Miners' Benevolent Association. By the 1880s, Polish, Hungarian, Lithuanian, and Italian immigrants began arriving in the United States and took jobs in the anthracite coal mines. In 1901, the number of strikes and lockouts across the United States was up to 3,012. The United States Steel Corporation broke a strike by the Amalgamated Association of Iron and Steel Workers. On May 12, 1902, over 140,000 anthracite coal miners across the districts of Wyoming, Lehigh, and Schuykill, in Pennsylvania, walked off their jobs. On May 16, 1902, the strike was made permanent by a vote of United Mine Workers (UMW) delegates. On October 11, 1902, Secretary of War Elihu Root and J. P. Morgan met secretly to propose a solution that called for a presidential commission to review the facts and offer a solution. The commission would be called by the mine operators. On October 13, 1902, J. P. Morgan gave President Roosevelt the proposal himself. On October 16, 1902, the White House announced the strike settled and the miners went back to work. In August 1902, the Western Federation of Miners (WFM) began organizing smelters in Colorado City but those who joined were fired by the Standard Oil refining company that employed those workers. In February 1903, the WFM went on strike against two other mills along with the Standard. In April 1903, Citizens' Alliances is formed by Colorado businessmen. In August 1903, the WFM struck the Cripple Creek district mines.

Colorado Governor James H. Peabody ordered the Colorado National Guard under Sherman Bell into Colorado City. In January 1905, twenty-one people met in Chicago secretly where they drafted the Industrial Union Manifesto. In June 1905, the Industrial Workers of the World (IWW, also known as "Wobblies") was formed at a convention in Chicago. On December 30, 1905, Harry Orchard killed the former Idaho Governor at his Caldwell home with a bomb. In December 1906, in Schenectady, New York, General Electric workers held a sit-down strike. Wobblies organized strikes in Bridgeport,

Connecticut and Paterson, New Jersey. In 1902, hat manufacturer Dietrich Lowe in Danbury, Connecticut, refused to recognize the United Hatters of North America. His workers went on strike, scabs were hired, and the striking workers boycotted Lowe's hats. In February 1908, the US Supreme Court ruled that the Sherman Antitrust Act covered organized labor as well as business and that the hatters restrained trade in violation of the US Constitution. The National Founders' Association and the National Association of Manufacturers (NAM) advocated for the "open-shop" workplace in opposition to the union members only "closed shop" workplace. Some employers used welfare capitalism and provided services and benefits to their employees, such as the Filene Cooperative Association Council at Filene's Department Store. Scientific management was based on <u>differential piece rate</u>, rewarding the most productive workers and driving away the least productive workers with pay raises and decreases, <u>motion study</u>, observing each minute in detail it takes to complete each aspect of a task, and <u>time study</u>, stopwatch measurements. Scientific management removes all individual intelligence and creativity from manual labor and is based on threats of wage cuts, temporary layoffs, fines, and dismissal. The Boston Arts and Crafts Society and the Society of Arts and Crafts led the American handicrafts movement by promoting craft guilds and the Gothic-style art and architecture of the Middle Ages. In 1903, the Women's Trade Union League (WTUL) was formed in Boston.

From 1897 to 1904, 1,800 companies turned into 157 during the Great Merger Movement. In the 1900s, the five approaches developed by Americans to control big business were as follows: the laissez-faire (do nothing) approach, the socialist public ownership approach, antitrust laws, regulations, and compensation through corporate taxation. In 1901, E. H. Harriman of the Union Pacific Railroad and James J. Hill of the Great Northern Railroad, with the support of James Stillman, Jacob Schiff, and J. P. Morgan, wanted control of the Chicago, Burlington, and Quincy (CB&Q) Railroad lines. The result was a battle for the Northern Pacific Railroad and the creation of the Northern Securities Company. On February 19, 1902, the US justice department announced an antitrust lawsuit against Northern Securities Company. On February 22, 1902, President Roosevelt and J. P. Morgan confronted each other on the antitrust issue. In 1904, the Supreme Court ruled that the Northern Securities Company was in violation of the Sherman Antitrust Act. In 1905, President Roosevelt ordered the federal government to investigate Standard Oil. In August 1906, the federal government found the Standard Oil Company of Indiana guilty of 1,462 federal violations and took the company to court. In November 1906, the federal government filed a lawsuit to dissolve the Standard Oil Company of New Jersey. By 1907, at least eight states took action against Standard Oil. In 1911, the Supreme Court ordered the Standard Oil Company of New Jersey broken up. In 1906, the Pure Food and Drug Act and the Meat-Inspection Act were passed by Congress and signed into law by President Roosevelt. In 1891, the Forest Reserve Act was passed by congress and signed into law by President Benjamin Harrison. In 1892, the Sierra Club was founded. In 1902, Congress passed the Newlands Act and President Roosevelt signed it into law. In 1905, the US Forest Service is established. On March 4, 1907, President Roosevelt signed the Agricultural Appropriation Act into law, after establishing twenty more national forests. In August 1907, President Roosevelt gave his "Malefactors of Great Wealth" speech in Provincetown, Massachusetts. On November 4, 1907, Elbridge Gary and Henry Clay Frick of US Steel discussed a proposal with President Roosevelt to end the Panic of 1907.

The "New South" of urbanization and industrialization, young whites were less tolerant of African Americans, young African Americans who were never enslaved, the African American middle class of landowners and business owners, and upper-class whites. Racist books (such as *The Negro a Beast* and *The Negro: A Menace to American Civilization)* along with race riots in New Orleans in July 1900 (where Robert Charles killed seven people and wounded twenty before being killed by a police officer, in New York City's Tenderloin district in August 1900, in Evansville, Indiana in 1903, in Atlanta in September 1906, and in Springfield, Illinois, in August 1908) had contributed to intense hatred of African Americans and toward white supremacy. Segregation in the Southern states meant Jim Crow laws while segregation in the Northern states consisted of a milder version of Jim Crow laws. Black residential districts, such as the Tenderloin and San Juan Hill (New York), Central Avenue (Cleveland), and etc., had difficulty getting and keeping jobs and joining unions. The approaches to segregation were the conservative approach advocated in 1895 in the Atlanta Compromise in which African Americans submit to white supremacy and focus on educational and economic progress. The progressive approach advocated in 1903 in *The Souls of Black Folk* in which an elite group of educated African Americans led the entire black community. This approach led to the formation of African American settlement houses, such as Boston's Robert Gould Shaw House, Manhattan's Lincoln House, Atlanta's Neighborhood Union, Hampton, Virginia's Locust Street Settlement, Indianapolis' Hanner House, and Louisville's Plymouth Settlement House. In 1905, the Niagara Movement was formed and led to the establishment of the National Association for the Advancement of Colored People (NAACP). Then there was the more radical approach advocated by the International Migration Society and the African Methodist Episcopal Church in which African Americans simply just leave the United States and go to Africa. In 1901, President Roosevelt invited Booker T. Washington to a White House dinner, only to face instant outrage from Southerners. In 1906, after the Brownsville, Texas, rampage, 170 African American US Army soldiers were dishonorably discharged by President Roosevelt. When they were eventually allowed to appeal to an army panel to reenlist, only fourteen went back into service. For dealing with Native Americans, the approach was not segregation but assimilation. In 1887, the Dawes Severality Act (General Allotment Act) was passed to assimilate Native Americans into white American culture and distribute their collectively-owned lands to individual Native Americans and whites. In 1903, the US Supreme Court's ruling in Lone Wolf vs. Hitchcock approved of the federal government's ability to open Native American tribal lands to exploitation. In 1906, the Burke Act was passed and made it so that a Native American receiving allotted lands had to wait twenty-five years to become a US citizen or until the secretary of the interior determined that Native American competent. Immigration restriction was another approach to segregation. Through the Immigration Restriction League, the targets were eastern and southern Europeans and Asians. In 1882, the Chinese Exclusion Act was passed by congress and signed into law by President Chester A. Arthur to make it difficult for Chinese people to immigrate and become citizens. In 1902, it was renewed by President Roosevelt. In 1903, the Anarchist Exclusion Act was passed by congress and signed into law by President Roosevelt to keep anarchists and "undesirables" out of the country. In 1903, the number of Japanese immigrants was 19,968, with the majority living in California. In 1906, the San Francisco School Board ordered Asian students segregated. President Roosevelt worked out the Gentleman's Agreement of 1907 with Japan. The Immigration Act of 1907 gave the President authorization to stop any immigration "to the detriment of labor conditions," doubled the entrance fee for immigrants, and set up an immigration investigation commission. Eugenics was a more extreme form of segregation that was promoted in Cold Spring Harbor, Long Island, at the Eugenics Record Office. American eugenics focused mainly on stopping mentally insane people from reproducing. In 1907, Indiana passed a law to sterilize mental hospital inmates and the Indiana idea spread to other states, including California. In 1910, after leaving office, Theodore Roosevelt supported the Eugenics Movement.

On December 17, 1903, at 10:35 a.m., the Wright brothers took flight with their Flyer I twin-engine biplane at Kitty Hawk, North Carolina. In twelve seconds, it flew 120 feet, with Orville as the pilot. In 1908, they held a public declaration of the airplane in Fort Myers, Florida. In 1909, Wilbur Wright flew around the Statue of Liberty. In 1910, the first long-distance flight took place from Albany to New York City. In 1911, a forty-nine-day flight cross-country from New York to California was made. In 1914, the first scheduled commercial flights took place. For ground transportation, the advancements were the Otis elevator, street railways, pneumatic tires, bicycles, and automobiles. At first, automobiles were so expensive that only the super wealthy could afford one. Counties in Pennsylvania and West Virginia banned cars from country roads. Near Sacramento, California, farmers dug ditches across roads to block traffic. Rural

Americans used broken glass, tacks, logs, chains, cables, barbed wire, horsewhips, and gunfire to stop automobiles and their drivers. In Minnetonka, Minnesota, a farmer shot a chauffeur in the back.

By 1900, most states imposed speed limits up to twenty-five miles per hour (mph). By 1907, the United States has surpassed Europe as the world's leading automobile manufacturer. In 1908, the Model T was introduced and General Motors was founded. In 1909, 9 percent of car owners in Maryland and 15 percent of car owners in Washington, DC, were women. In 1910, the first mass-production plant was opened in Highland Park, Michigan. "Traffic jam" became a commonly used term. In 1911, the Indianapolis 500 took place for the first time. In 1914, 5 percent of car owners in Tucson, Arizona, and 15 percent of car owners in Los Angeles were women. The city of Cleveland installed the first traffic light on Euclid Avenue. In 1915, motorists were staging their own drag races. Every state now required motor vehicles to be registered. In 1916, the cost of a new Model T dropped to $360 and sales jumped to 377,036. Farmers began buying automobiles and by 1920, there would be over two million automobiles on farms. In 1903, Theodore Roosevelt and King Edward VII traded messages using wireless telegraph (radio). In 1904, a transatlantic news service was set up by the Marconi Company. Ships at sea were sending distress signals by wireless telegraph. On April 15, 1912, wireless transmissions broadcast the tragedy of the Titanic sinking disaster. In 1914, there were 10 million telephones in the United States, one for every ten Americans. Over a half a million phonographs (record player) were shipped. Space, time, matter, and self were central to the concept of modernism. In 1890, *The Principles of Psychology* was published. In 1905, the special theory of relativity was introduced. In 1911, the Association of American Painters and Sculptors (AAPS) was founded by modernist artists.

The Mind of Primitive Man was published. From February 17 to March 15, 1913, at 10:00 p.m., the Armory Show displayed modernist art to the general public. In 1916, the general theory of relativity was introduced and *The Passing of the Great Race* was published. In 1915, average working hours for unionized tradesmen dropped to 44.8. Average factory wages rose to $568. By the 1910s, the new progressive middle class now had more time and money to spend on pleasure. The World's Fair led to the establishment of amusement parks. Vaudeville theaters and dance halls were another form of entertainment. In the 1910s, New York City had five hundred dance halls and over a hundred dancing schools. Ragtime, Hawaiian, and Jazz were popular forms of music. Professional sports such as horse racing, car racing, and baseball were becoming more popular. In 1901, the American League was formed. In 1903, the first World Series was played. Major League Baseball attracted an audience of both men and women, and in 1909, turnout reached a peak of 7.2 million. Baseball stadiums were being built: 1909 was Shibe Park in Philadelphia, 1912 was Fenway Park in Boston, and 1913 was Ebbets Field in Brooklyn. In 1904, the first nickelodeon theater opened in a storefront on Diamond Street in Pittsburgh. This idea spread to Cincinnati, Philadelphia, Rochester, Dallas, Chicago, and Baltimore. By 1910, there were about ten thousand nickelodeons throughout the United States. Among the silent films shown at nickelodeons were *Oh! That Limburger: The Story of a Piece of Cheese, Cowboys and Indians, Uncle Tom's Cabin*, etc. In the 1910s, nickelodeons were being replaced with larger, palace-like theaters such as the Princess in Milwaukee. They were located in suburbs and charged up to twenty-five cents admission. In 1913, *Traffic in Souls* and *The Inside of the White Slave Traffic* were multireel films that commanded large audiences. By 1915, after the release of *The Birth of a Nation*, movies became an acceptable entertainment. In 1912, Margaret Sanger published the *What Every Girl Should Know* newspaper articles. In 1915, the birth control movement began. In the 1910s, the first-wave feminist movement began in Greenwich Village, New York. In 1912, Heterodoxy was founded by twenty-five women. In 1914, the Feminist Alliance was formed and two meetings were held at Cooper's Union on the topic "What Is Feminism?" The radical journal, *The Masses*, published answers to that question. In 1911, a New York State law took effect that prohibited liquor sales in dancing schools and made it difficult to have dancing in saloons. In 1906, the Chicago police were given authority to closedown certain kinds of movies showing criminal and immoral scenes. In 1907, Chicago enacted the first film censorship ordinance banning movies that are immoral or obscene and any films shown required a permit. In 1909, a film censorship commission was established in Chicago to carry out the law. On December 24, 1908, New York City Mayor George McClellan closed theaters temporarily. Afterward, theaters owners would need licenses. The National Board of Review was established. In 1914, when Margaret Sanger began publishing the *Woman Rebel* magazine, she was indicted in August 1914 for violating the 1873 Comstock Act's ban on mailing materials that are "obscene, lewd, or lascivious." By the own legal promise she made in court, she was released but never showed up in court, left her family, and fled to Canada and then to Europe. In 1915, her husband, William Sanger, published her contraception pamphlet "Family Limitation" and was convicted. The National Birth Control League was organized. In 1916, the charges against Margaret Sanger were dropped.

During the Taft and Wilson administrations, more progressive laws were enacted that ether extended or stopped those of the Roosevelt administration. In 1910, Congress passed the White Slave Traffic Act (Mann Act) to outlaw interstate prostitution. The Bureau of Investigation was given responsibility to enforce the Mann Act. In 1912, the Children's Bureau is established in the Department of Commerce and Labor. In 1913, Congress passed the Webb-Kenyon Act, vetoed by President Taft, but overridden by Congress. During the controversy involving Secretary of the Interior Richard Achilles Ballinger and Chief Forester Gifford Pinchot, President Taft fired the latter for undermining the former's policies. Both Presidents Taft and Wilson did little to nothing for African and Native Americans. In 1894, Congress passed the Wilson-Gorman Act that included a 2 percent tax on yearly incomes over four thousand dollars, which was declared unconstitutional by the Supreme Court. In 1909, Congress approved the Sixteenth Amendment to the Constitution and was ratified in 1913. On October 3, 1913, the Underwood Tariff Act was passed and lowered tariff rates from 40 percent to 25 percent. In 1914, Congress enacted a 1 percent tax on yearly incomes from four thousand dollars to twenty thousand dollars. Even larger incomes had a surtax. In 1916, income tax rates were raised and the first permanent inheritance tax enacted by Congress included a 10 percent levy on estates over five million dollars. In 1916, the Keating-Owen Child Labor Act is enacted by Congress but is struck down in 1918 as unconstitutional by the Supreme Court in *Hammer v. Dagenhart*. In 1914, the National Consumers' League helped to passed the La Follette-Peters Act mandating an eight-hour day for most female workers in Washington, DC. In 1915, the La Follette Seaman's Act was passed regulating American sailors' hours and working conditions. In 1916, the Adamson Act was passed mandating an eight-hour day for railroad workers. In 1913, the Federal Reserve Act was passed by Congress and signed into law by President Wilson to stabilize the currency and banking systems. On April 8, 1913, the Seventeenth Amendment to the Constitution was ratified to allow for the direct election of US Senators by popular vote. On September 26, 1914, the Federal Trade Commission Act was passed. On October 15, 1914, the Clayton Antitrust Act was passed. On January 9–10, 1915, the Women's Peace Party (WPP) was founded. On April 26, 1915, the Treaty of London was signed. On April 28–May 1, 1915, the International Congress of Women was held in the Netherlands. On June 17, 1915, the League to Enforce Peace (LEP) was established. In 1916, the Council of National Defense (CND) established a Women's Committee. In 1917, the National Women's Party (NWP) began picketing in front of the White House. In 1917, the Eighteenth Amendment to the Constitution prohibiting the sale, manufacturing, and distribution of alcoholic beverages is passed by Congress, ratified by the states, and becomes law in 1920. In 1918, the Nineteenth Amendment to the Constitution giving women the right to vote is passed by Congress, ratified by the states, and becomes law in 1920.

In March 1914, the *Srbobran* newspaper went into detail that Archduke Franz Ferdinand was definitely coming to Bosnia and Herzegovina to observe military maneuvers. On Thursday, June 25, 1914, he arrived to attend two days of Austrian military maneuvers. On Friday, June 26, 1914, he was a companion for his wife Sophie on a shopping expedition in the Sarajevo Bazaars. On Saturday, June 27, 1914, he hosted Mayor Fehim Effendi, Bosnian officials, and

Catholic, Orthodox, and Muslim leaders at the Hotel Bosnia in Ilidža, six miles west of Sarajevo, for a banquet. On Sunday, June 28, 1914, he woke up in his Hotel Bosnia suite surrounded by Persian carpets, Arabesque lamp figurines, and Turkish single-edged and curved swords called scimitars. Among the conspirators who were planning to murder the archduke were Nedjelko Cabrinovic, Gavrilo Princip, and Trifko Grabež. Milan Ciganović offered his stash of explosives, Major Tankosić gave them four Browning revolvers, ammunition, 150 dinars (cash), and cyanide for the assassin to commit suicide afterward. Milan Ciganović and Major Tankosić were members of the Black Hand nationalist group that had built an underground tunnel to smuggle people into Austria. On May 26, 1914, Gavrilo Princip, Nedjelko Cabrinovic, and Trifko Grabež arrived at Šabac. Serbian Army Officer Major Popovitch provided Nedjelko Cabrinovic with papers and instructed him to cross the border to Zvornik, where he would be driven to Tuzla, and there he would get on a train to Sarajevo. Gavrilo Princip and Trifko Grabež crossed the Drina River near Lješnica and into Bosnia where they arrived at Priboj and met schoolmaster Narodna Odbrana and member Veljko Chubrilovitch.

Before reaching the Austrian checkpoint at Lopare, Gavrilo Princip and Trifko Grabež left their weapons, bombs, and poison in a peasant's cart. They were reunited with Nedjelko Cabrinovic in Tuzla where they gave their dangerous cargo to Misko Jovanovic who, in turn, hid them in his attic. Nedjelko Cabrinovic, Gavrilo Princip, and Trifko Grabež came to Sarajevo where the former two were taken by Danilo Ilitch and the latter by his own family. In Tuzla, Danilo Ilitch presented a pack of Stephanie cigarettes to Misko Jovanovic and asked him to take the dangerous cargo, hidden in a box of sugar, to meet him in Doboj. On Sunday, June 28, 1914, in the Vladjinitch pastry shop, Danilo Ilitch returned the dangerous cargo to Gavrilo Princip, Nedjelko Cabrinovic, and Trifko Grabež where the first conspirator took a pistol, the second a bomb, and the third both. Meanwhile, Archduke Franz Ferdinand was getting ready by dressing in an Austrian cavalry general's uniform: a blue tunic over black trousers with red stripes and gold collar with three silver stars. Sophie wore a very delicate white veil, white hat, with a rose bouquet in her red sash. At 9:20 a.m., their companion was Governor Potiorek as they traveled on a train from Ilidža to Sarajevo. After reviewing local troops together, they got into an open car behind the mayor and police chief's car and in front of staff cars in the imperial motorcade that would proceed down the Appel Quai along the right side of the road to town hall and down the other side on the way back. Danilo Ilitch recruited Vaso Chubrilovitch, Cvjetko Popovitch, and Mehmedbashitch. Danilo Ilitch positioned himself across the Appel Quai from the Cumurja Bridge along with Cvjetko Popovitch. Mehmedbashitch, Vaso Chubrilovitch, and Nedjelko Cabrinovic were positioned along the Appel Quai on the side of the river. The first two had pistols and the third had a fuse bomb. Gavrilo Princip waited at the Lateiner Bridge with his revolver. Trifko Grabež waited near the Kaiser Bridge with a pistol and bomb. The first two didn't do a thing when the motorcade passed. The third threw his bomb at the archduke's car as it increased in speed. It bounced off the back hood and went underneath the staff car behind and detonated, damaging the car and wounding people in the process.

Nedjelko Cabrinovic was taken in by police officers after he jumped into the river. The motorcade then proceeded at a higher speed to discourage other assassination attempts. At the town hall, Sophie met with Muslim women while the archduke himself heard public speeches by Mayor Fehim Effendi. Before leaving the town hall, the archduke decided he wanted to visit the Garrison Hospital before going to the governor's konak for a luncheon. The motorcade would move at high speed down the Appel Quai before reaching the Franz-Josef Strasse. Trifko Grabež remained at Kaiser Bridge while Gavrilo Princip moved to position himself in front of the Moritz Schiller spice emporium. The motorcade was now arranged with a police car first, the mayor's second, the archduke's car and three staff cars. Count Harrach rode along the left running board of the archduke's car. As the first three cars turn right onto Franz-Josef Strasse, Governor Potiorek in the archduke's car ordered the chauffeur to turn back. The chauffeur hit the brakes and after he did, Gavrilo Princip stepped in with his Browning revolver and fired one shot at Archduke Franz Ferdinand's neck and Sophie's stomach. The Archduke's car turned around and sped toward the governor's konak. At 11:30 a.m., the Archduke Franz Ferdinand and Sophie died from their wounds. The assassination resulted in the July Crisis among European nations Austria, Russia, France, Great Britain, and Germany that ended with the beginning of World War I.

On August 3, 1914, President Wilson gives a press conference about the United States remaining neutral in the war. On January 15, 1915, a Commercial Agency Agreement is signed between J. P. Morgan and Company and the British government. On February 4, 1915, the German government announced it would use the submarine (U-boat) to retaliate against Great Britain's restrictive measures. In February 1915, the British launched an assault against Turkey.

In April 1915, Italy joined the Allied powers. From January 1915 to April 1917, J. P. Morgan bought over three billion dollars' worth of Allied goods. On May 7, 1915, the British passenger ship, *Lusitania* was struck by the U-20 German submarine off the Irish coast. 128 Americans were killed as a result. President Wilson and Department of State Counselor Robert Lansing sent three notes to the German government. On May 13, 1915, the first note declared firmly Americans right to travel on merchant ships as passengers, demanding Germany deny responsibility for attacking merchant ships and pledge not to attack commercial ships with submarines. On June 9, 1915, the second note dismisses arguments by Germany stating the British blockade as being an illegal, cruel, and deadly attack on civilians and that the Lusitania was carrying war supplies. On July 21, 1915, the third note was an ultimatum stating that anymore sinkings would be regarded as "deliberately unfriendly." On August 19, 1915, the British merchant ship Arabic was struck by a torpedo from a German submarine and sank. Two Americans were killed. In November 1915, the American International Corporation (AIC) was founded. In 1915, Treasury Secretary William Gibbs McAdoo urged President Wilson to endorse a Morgan-backed half-billion-dollar loan on the British behalf and President Wilson rejected. The Plattsburg Movement was formed, beginning in New York and expanding to Illinois and California for the training of an officer corps. The Naval Consulting Board (NCB) was established. On February 3, 1916,

President Wilson called for the building of a large US Navy. On February 22, 1916, the House-Grey Memorandum was proposed. In February 1916, President Wilson replaced his Secretary of War Lindley M. Garrison with Newton D. Baker because of the former's support for a new Continental Army. In March 1916, troops were dispatched by President Wilson to protect Americans living near the Mexican border from Pancho Villa and his rebels that were conducting raids. On March 24, 1916, the French steamer *Sussex* was sunk by a German submarine. Two Americans were killed. On April 18, 1916, the United States threatened to cut diplomatic relations with Germany if they continued to attack merchant and passenger ships with submarines. On May 4, 1916, Germany issued a pledge renouncing surprise attacks on merchant and passenger ships. In May and June 1916, as General John J. Pershing and the regular army tried to track down Pancho Villa and his rebels, 110,000 US National Guardsmen were mobilized by President Wilson. In May 1916, on Fifth Avenue in New York City, 135,000 Preparedness supporters marched in a twelve-hour procession. President Wilson was unwilling to endorse the views of the American Union Against Militarism (AUAM). On June 3, 1916, 350,000 Preparedness marchers took to the streets in 10 cities. In June 1916, a British-French economic conference was held. The National Defense Act created the Council of National Defense (CND). The Democratic National Convention was held where President Wilson's slogan, "He Kept Us Out of War," was established. The Dick Act was passed. In August 1916, as part of a three-year building program, the US congress got funds to construct new battleships. In October 1916, the CND Advisory Council began to take inventory of scientific and industrial resources in the United States and started a network of advisory and information-gathering bodies at state and local level working through chambers of commerce. On December 18, 1916, President Wilson made his peace note public. On a Midwest speaking tour, President Wilson endorsed expanding the navy and military reform. American exports to Great Britain and France rose to almost six billions dollars. The Naval Appropriations Act was passed.

On January 8–9, 1917, German General Erich Ludendorff and naval leaders pushed the Kaiser to endorse a program abandoning the Sussex pledge. On January 22, 1917, President Wilson gave his "Peace Without Victory" speech to a joint US Congress session stating an end to military and economic alliances, limiting firearms and munitions production, freedom of the seas, the peoples' right to choose what kind of government to live under, and an international organization to ensure peace. On January 31, 1917, German Ambassador to the US Count Johann von Bernstorff delivered the submarine warfare proclamation to Secretary of State Robert Lansing. On February 1, 1917, the unrestricted submarine warfare campaign began. On February 3, 1917, President Wilson severed diplomatic relations with Germany. In February 1917, as President Wilson authorized arming American merchant ships, the *Zimmermann Telegram* was released, revealing a German-Mexican plan to take back US territory in the Southwest if Mexico joined the war. On March 8–17, 1917, the February Revolution occurred in the Russian Empire that resulted in Czar Nicholas II's abdication, the creation and establishment of the Russian Republic and Provisional Government, ruling alongside the Petrograd Soviet of Workers' and Soldiers' Deputies. On March 16–18, 1917, three Americans ships were sunk by German submarines. On March 20, 1917, President Wilson held a cabinet meeting and then called for a meeting of Congress on April 2. In March 1917, the American Protective League (APL) was established. It went on to recruit three hundred thousand members mostly from upperclass citizens.

On April 2, 1917, President Wilson entered the House chamber of the US Congress on a rainy evening to give a thirty-six-minute speech stressing the German government as militaristic, elimination of the German "war autocracy," distinguishing the German people from the German state, comparing to show differences between the "democratic" Allied powers' governments with the "autocratic" Germany, America's own reasons for going to war, America's cooperation with the Allied powers, and the creation of a democratic, American-dominated new world order. On April 6, 1917, the US Congress passed President Wilson's war declaration, eighty-two to six in the Senate and 375 to 50 in the House. After April 6, 1917, employers and government officials began to recruit women. On May 4, 1917, six American destroyers arrived in Queenstown, Ireland. On May 18, 1917, the Selective Service Act was passed in both houses of Congress. On Tuesday, June 5, 1917, about ten million men between twenty-one to thirty registered for the Selective Service. On June 15, 1917, the Espionage Act was passed. In June 1917, the army called for 687,000 men added to the nearly 220,000 men it already had. City authorities and businessmen in Bisbee, Arizona gathered up striking IWW copper workers, put them in railroad cars, took them to the desert, and stranded them without water. On July 4, 1917, a Sixteenth Regiment battalion marched through Paris, France. On July 20, 1917, lottery drawings were held to begin draftee selection. In July 1917, the War Industries Board (WIB) was established. On August 10, 1917, the Lever Act was passed and established the Food and Fuel Administrations. On August 23, 1917, Twenty-Fourth Infantry soldiers marched on Houston, Texas, after local police beat a black soldier. In August 1917, the American Alliance for Labor and Democracy was created as a front by the AFL for the Committee on Public Information (CPI). By September 1, 1917, construction workers built facilities to house four hundred thousand new soldiers. On September 5, 1917, using the Espionage Act, federal officials raided the IWW. In September 1917, President Wilson created the President's Mediation Commission (PMC). In October 1917, the Trading with the Enemy Act was passed.

On November 2–3, 1917, the First Division suffered the first American combat deaths. On November 7–8, 1917, the October Revolution ended the Russian Provisional Government, started the Russian Civil War, and created the Soviet Union. In November 1917, the Supreme Allied War Council was created. President Wilson addressed AFL's annual convention in Buffalo. On December 26, 1917, the United States Railroad Administration (USRA) was created. In 1917, the War Revenue Act was passed and set up the Liberty Loans. German submarines destroyed over six million tons of shipping. The rail-coal crisis occurred.

On January 8, 1918, President Wilson made his Fourteen Points statement:

1. Evacuation and restoration of Belgium.
2. Germany returns Alsace-Lorraine to France and leaves.
3. The right to national self-determination for the peoples ruled by the Austro-Hungarian, Turkish, and German empires.
4. The creation of a Polish state.
5. Independence and territorial consistency guaranteed for the restored southeastern European small states.
6. German forces must evacuate Russian territory.
7. Elimination of secret treaties and etc. among the nations.
8. The high seas open to all commerce without interference.
9. Elimination of reduction of tariffs and etc. to free international trade.
10. Limiting the firearms and munitions productions.
11. Considering the interest of subject peoples when resolving disagreement over colonial matters in a manner that treats all rivals fair and just.
12. A general association of nations.

In January 1918, the US Congress changed the draft age from eighteen to forty-five. French and British instructors were training up to 175,000 American soldiers. On March 3, 1918, the Treaty of Brest-Litovsk was signed on the Eastern Front. On March 21, 1918, General Erich Ludendorff launched the first attack against the Allied lines. In March 1918, the Federal Control Act was passed. On April 8, 1918, the National War Labor Board (NWLB) was created by executive order. On May 16, 1918, the Sedition Act was passed. On May 20, 1918, the Overman Act was passed. In May 1918, 166 IWW officials and organizers were indicted by a federal grand jury.

The United States Housing Corporation (USHC) was created. The Division of Negro Economics (DNE) was created in the Department of Labor. At Cantigny, Chateau-Thierry, and Belleau Wood, thirty miles from Paris, American troops fought for three weeks along the Marne River and Belleau Wood, and lost 4,500 lives trying to repel a German advance. On July 18, 1918, at the Aisne-Marne, German units were pushed back by American First and Second Division troops.

American Third Division troops were along the Marne River holding off repeated enemy attacks. The total number of American soldiers were 310,000. The pro-war editorial *Close Ranks* was published. The US congress established a Women in Industry Service in the Department of Labor. President Wilson ordered General John J. Pershing to detach units to the Archangel region, six hundred miles north of Moscow. 144 Americans were killed in combat, seventy-eight from disease, and 305 were wounded. He also ordered troops sent to the port of Vladivostok. On September 12, 1918, at St. Mihiel, five hundred thousand American troops led an assault with one hundred thousand French troops in which German forces were pushed back fifteen miles south of Verdun. On September 26, 1918, at Meuse-Argonne, 2,700 German guns opened fire. American First Army troops moved forward. On September 27, 1918, President Wilson gave an address reaffirming the principles of the Fourteen Points. On October 3, 1918, the German chancellor sent a message to President Wilson asking for an armistice based on the Fourteen Points. On October 4 and October 14, General Pershing renewed the advance. On October 24, 1918, the Eighty-Eighth Division fought Germans and ninety men were lost. On November 1, 1918, the battle was beginning to reach its conclusion. On November 7, 1918, the Democratic Party lost control of the US Congress in the midterm elections. On November 11, 1918, at 5:00 a.m., the Armistice was signed. At 11:00 a.m, it became effective. On December 4, 1918, President Wilson gave his State of the Union speech warning against "the voices of humanity." In 1918, during the Spanish flu pandemic, the Eighty-Eighth Army Division lost 444 to influenza and pneumonia. The US government took over control of the telegraph lines from the Western Union Company. In Bridgeport, Connecticut, employees of the Remington Arms Company went on strike. In the trials of 1918, over one hundred Wobblies were convicted and sent to federal prisons.

On January 18, 1919, the Paris Peace Conference opened. The next day, deliberations began. Between February 15 to March 1919, Edward House was President Wilson's emissary in Paris while the latter came back to the United States. In February 1919, the Seattle General Strike occurred. On March 2, 1919, thirty-nine US Senators issued a Round Robin statement opposing the Treaty of Versailles. The Soviet government established the Communist International (Comintern). The NWLB put an end to all operations. Between March to June 1919, the Council of Four met over 140 times at President Wilson's Paris residence. On April 28, 1919, a homemade explosive device was mailed to Seattle Mayor Ole Hanson but failed to detonate.

The next day, Georgia Senator Thomas W. Hardwick's maid lost her hands upon opening a parcel addressed to her employer. On May 1, 1919 (May Day), in Cleveland, Ohio, during a left wing parade of unionists, socialists, communists, and anarchists, riots occurred. In May 1919, the Germans received a draft version of the treaty. On June 28, 1919, the Germans signed the treaty. Between July, to August 1919, the balloting took place as more workers joined the National Committee for Organizing Iron and Steel Workers (NCOISW) and became more militant. On July 8, 1919, President Wilson arrived in New York harbor on the USS *George Washington* with the Treaty of Versailles and the League of Nations constitution. On July 10, 1919, President Wilson presented the Treaty of Versailles to the US senate and gave a speech focusing on the League of Nations. On July 27, 1919, on a beach in Chicago, a black child who accidently stepped over a race line was killed by white teenagers. In July 1919, the NCOISW's demand list included:

1. Union recognition
2. Elimination of employment practices subjected to the individual worker's will and judgment
3. Reduction of the seventy-two-hour workweek
4. Wage increases that would guarantee an American living standard

On August 1, 1919, the General Intelligence Division (GID) was established in the US justice department. On September 1, 1919, the Communist Party of the United States was formed. On September 4, 1919, President Wilson began a presidential speaking tour starting in Columbus, Ohio, on to Indianapolis, St. Louis, Kansas City, Des Moines, St. Paul, Minneapolis, Bismarck, Helena, Coeur d' Alene, Spokane, Seattle, Portland, San Francisco, Los Angeles, and San Diego to get support for the Treaty and League of Nations. On September 9, 1919, the Boston Police Strike occurred. On September 22, 1919, 250,000 steelworkers from Colorado to New York walked off their jobs. In September 1919, in Helena, Montana, President Wilson discussed racial violence in a foreign policy speech. On October 5, 1919, President Wilson had a massive stroke that affected his memory and speech and left him paralyzed and in seclusion for five weeks. In October 1919, *The Economic Consequences of the Peace* was published and attacked the Treaty of Versailles. On November 7, 1919, the Palmer Raids began when federal agents targeted the Union of Russian Workers (URW), with the assistance of New York City Police, and arrested two hundred people even though they only had arrest warrants for twenty-seven. On November 19, 1919, democratic senators, at President Wilson's instruction, voted against the treaty because of Senator Henry Cabot Lodge's reservations. The US Senate then voted against the treaty thirty-eight to fifty-three. In November 1919, in Centralia, Washington, American Legion post members marched on the IWW local hall. The Wobblies killed several legionaries. In 1919, labor union membership increased to four million.

On January 8, 1920, the NCOISW declared the strike over. On March 19, 1920, President Wilson instructed democratic senators to reject the treaty. Twenty-one democratic senators voted for the treaty with the reservations from Senator Lodge. But enough Wilson-loyal democrats ensured the treaty's defeat in a forty-nine to thirty-five majority. On May 7, 1920, the Treaty of Versailles was presented at the Trianon Palace in Versailles. In August 1920, the Ottoman Empire signed the Treaty of Sevres. On November 2, 1920, during the presidential election, the Democratic Party ran James M. Cox for president and Franklin Delano Roosevelt for vice president. The

Republican Party ran Warren G. Harding for president and Calvin Coolidge for vice president. The Harding-Coolidge ticket won in a landslide. On July 2, 1921, the US congress declared the war over after President Harding signed the Knox-Porter Resolution. On Black Tuesday, October 29, 1929, the stock market crashed, which led to the Great Depression.

On November 8, 1932, Franklin Delano Roosevelt (FDR) was elected President and proposed "a new deal." The majority of surviving progressive activists opposed FDR and the New Deal. He was criticized for going too far and not far enough increasing the federal government's size, intervening in the economy, and serving organized labor. He abandoned key elements of progressivism, such as the personal transformation of individual Americans. On December 5, 1933, he supported the Twenty-First Amendment to the Constitution repealing Prohibition.

Other concerns about FDR and the New Deal were that some aspects, if you look carefully, had striking similarities to Italian Fascism and German National Socialism:

1. FDR's "fireside chats" and Adolf Hitler's "Nuremberg rallies."
2. The National Recovery Administration (NRA)'s Blue Eagle campaign and Nazi Germany's Winter Relief organization.
3. The Arthurdale project of the US Subsistence Homesteads Division and the Ramersdorf settlement of Nazi Germany's Commission for Settlement Projects.
4. The reclamation of the Pontine Marshes (Agro Pontino) in Fascist Italy, the programs of the Tennessee Valley Authority (TVA), and the construction of the Autobahn in Nazi Germany.
5. The Civilian Conservation Corps (CCC) was structured in a paramilitary fashion.
6. Other New Deal organizations with similarities to Fascist Italy and Nazi Germany were the Federal Housing Administration (FHA) and the Federal Communications Commission (FCC).

Those who opposed FDR and the New Deal formed the conservative coalition while supporters, mostly city dwellers, formed the New Deal coalition. The Soviet Union entered World War II, after Operation Barbarossa (June 22 to December 5, 1941), the United States after the attack on Pearl Harbor (December 7, 1941), and the British Empire, and formed the Allied powers. On February 19, 1942, FDR signed Executive Order Number 9066 that authorized the relocation and internment of Japanese-Americans. World War II ended with the defeat of the Axis Powers, Nazi Germany and Fascist Italy. On June 26, 1945, the United Nations Charter was signed by fifty original members, including the United States. The atomic bombings of Hiroshima (August 6, 1945) and Nagasaki (August 9, 1945) in the Empire of Japan resulted in the signing the Instrument of Surrender on September 2, 1945. On October 24, 1945, the UN Charter was ratified by five permanent members, China, France, Russia, the United Kingdom, and the United States. In the years after World War II, the United States and the Soviet Union became enemies and fought the Cold War, lasting from 1947 to 1991, when the Soviet Union broke up.

During the Cold War period, from 1950 to 1956, was the second Red Scare that was known as McCarthyism. On May 17, 1954, Brown vs. Board of Education was decided and overturned the 1896 Plessy vs. Ferguson decision. Martin Luther King Jr. organized the Montgomery Bus Boycott from December 1, 1955, after the Rosa Parks incident, until December 26, 1956. In 1957, nine black students (Little Rock Nine) enrolled at Little Rock Central High School. The first Civil Rights Act was passed. In 1960, black students organized sit-in movements in Nashville and Greensboro. In January 1960, Massachusetts Senator John Fitzgerald Kennedy (JFK) announced his candidacy for president. On July 11, 1960, at the Democratic National Convention in Los Angeles he won the nomination and chose Texas Senator Lyndon B. Johnson (LBJ) as his running mate. The campaign issues were the Cold War, economic growth, public sector repair, and civil rights. In September 1960, JFK decided to run as a civil rights candidate while LBJ campaigned for white southerners. The Republican presidential nominee was

Vice President Richard Nixon. On September 25, 1960, the televised Kennedy-Nixon debates began. JFK won 49.7 percent of the popular vote. He won New York, Massachusetts, Pennsylvania, Michigan, New Jersey, and Illinois in the Northeast and Midwest, giving him 156 electoral votes. In the South, he won Texas, Louisiana, Arkansas, Alabama, North Carolina, South Carolina, and Georgia, giving him 81 electoral votes. He also won the border states of Maryland, Delaware, Missouri, West Virginia, Connecticut, Minnesota, etc. He won 303 electoral votes total. Vice President Nixon won 49.5 percent of the popular vote. He won Ohio, California, Florida, Virginia, and Tennessee. He won 219 electoral votes total. Some of the laws passed during JFK's administration would lay the foundation for the Great Society later. On September 22, 1961, the Juvenile Delinquency and Youth Offenses Control Act was passed. On March 15, 1962, the Manpower Development and Training Act was passed. On October 11, 1962, the Trade Expansion Act was passed. On Friday, November 22, 1963, in Dallas, Texas, JFK was assassinated and LBJ was immediately sworn in as president. On January 8, 1964, he gave his State of the Union address declaring a "war on poverty." In January 1964, Arizona Senator Barry Goldwater announced his candidacy for president. On February 1, 1964, LBJ puts Robert Sargent Shriver in charge of the Poverty Task Force. On June 2, 1964, Senator Goldwater defeated New York Governor Nelson Rockefeller in the California primary by sixty-eight thousand votes. On July 2, 1964, LBJ signed the Civil Rights Act into law.

In July 1964, the Republican National Convention was held at Cow Palace in San Francisco where Senator Goldwater chose New York congressman William E. Miller as his running mate and gave his "Extremism in Defense of Liberty" speech. Minnesota Senator Hubert Humphrey would become LBJ's running mate. On August 4, 1964, after 10:00 a.m. in the Gulf of Tonkin, the USS *Maddox* reported being under North Vietnamese torpedo attack, with the C. Turner Joy. The USS *Maddox* was in fact a spy ship, the USS *Maddox* and C. Turner Joy were in fact part of a covert operation organized by the United States and carried out by the South Vietnamese to bomb coastal targets in North Vietnam. The first attack reports were based on evidence regarded with disbelief by messages from the USS *Maddox* itself. On August 5, 1964, LBJ submitted the Gulf of Tonkin Resolution to the US Congress. On August 20, 1964, he signed the Economic Opportunity Act into law. He carried forty-four states and won 61 percent of the popular vote. Senator Goldwater won only Arizona, Mississippi, Louisiana, Alabama, Georgia, and South Carolina. In January 1965, twenty thousand US military personnel were serving in Vietnam to give combat instructions to the South Vietnamese Army. In February 1965, LBJ initiated Rolling Thunder. In March 1965, he started sending combat troops to South Vietnam. On April 11, 1965, the Elementary and Secondary Education Act was passed. On June 7, 1965, General William Westmoreland asked for large ground reinforcements. On July 28, 1965, LBJ ordered US troop strength increased in Vietnam to 125,000. On July 30, 1965, in Independence, Missouri, at Harry S. Truman's house, he signed the Social Security Amendments establishing Medicare and Medicaid into law. On August 5, 1965, he signed the Voting Rights Act into law. On August 10, 1965, he signed the Housing and Urban Development Act into law. On September 9, 1965, the Housing and Urban Development Department (HUD) was established. On April 11, 1968, he signed another Civil Rights Act into law involving housing. On June 28, 1968, he signed the Revenue and Expenditure Control Act into law.

On January 14, 1967, the first Human Be-In took place in Golden Gate Park, San Francisco. This was the beginning of the hippie counterculture movement. In June 1967, the Monterey International Pop Festival was held. Haight-Ashbury, San Francisco would become the center of the movement. On April 15, 1967, at Sheep Meadow, Central Park, New York, the Spring Mobilization Committee called an antiwar march where 60 people burned their draft cards. This was the beginning of the New Left political move-ment. In October 1967, Stop the Draft Week was held that ended in Arlington, Virginia with the March on the Pentagon. On February 21, 1965, Malcolm X was assassinated at the Audubon Ballroom in New York City. This was the beginning of the Black Power nationalist movement. The Watts riot began on August 11, 1965, and ended on

August 14, 1965, when the National Guard came in. 34 were killed, 1,072 were injured, 977 building were damaged and/or destroyed, and four thousand were arrested. In 1967, the Newark and Detroit riots occurred. The latter began on July 23, 1967, and ended on July 25, 1967, when Lieutenant General John L. Throckmorton began deploying 4,700 paratroopers to Detroit. Forty-three were killed, seven thousand arrested, 1,300 buildings were destroyed, and 2,700 businesses were looted. The Black Panthers Party was founded. In February 1966, Senator Fulbright held televised hearings on the Vietnam War. On March 2, 1967, Senator Robert F. Kennedy (RFK) gave a speech to stop the bombings in North Vietnam and to negotiate a compromise. On October 12, 1967, the New York Review published "A Call to Resist Illegitimate Authority," and signed by 121 intellectuals. On January 31, 1968, the Tet Offensive was launched. On February 3, 1968, Richard Nixon entered the New Hampshire primary. On March 12, 1968, 49 percent of New Hampshire Democratic voters wrote in LBJ's name and 42 percent marked in Minnesota Senator Eugene McCarthy. Richard Nixon won 79 percent of the New Hampshire Republican voters. On March 16, 1968, RFK announced his candidacy for president. On March 31, 1968, LBJ gave his "House Divided" speech, stating he would not run for reelection. On April 4, 1968, Martin Luther King Jr. was assassinated in Memphis, Tennessee. On April 17, 1968, at the Shoreham Hotel ballroom, before 1,700 supporters, Vice President Hubert Humphrey announced his candidacy for president. On May 28, 1968, Richard Nixon won the Oregon primary. In May 1968, RFK defeated Senator McCarthy in the Indiana and Nebraska primaries. In the Oregon primary, Senator McCarthy won 45 percent and RFK won 39 percent. On June 4, 1968, in the California primary, RFK won 46.3 percent and Senator McCarthy won 41.8 percent. RFK was assassinated walking through the kitchen of the Ambassador Hotel. On June 18, 1968, in the New York primary, Senator McCarthy won sixty-two delegates, Vice President Hubert Humphrey won twelve delegates, and RFK won thirty delegates. Richard Nixon won the Republican nomination and selects Maryland Governor Spiro Agnew as his running mate. On the issue of law and order,

Richard Nixon proposed to convict more criminals, wiretapping, and more pay for police officers. On the issue of race, he had Richard Whalen write a speech proposing to help blacks by encouraging private businesses to invest in black neighborhoods and hire black workers. During the Democratic National Convention held at the Chicago Amphitheater, the Battle of Chicago was fought between the yippies, the National Mobilization Committee to End the War in Vietnam (the Mobe), and the Chicago Police Department. Vice President Hubert Humphrey won the Democratic presidential nomination. On Thursday, August 29, 1968, Maine Senator Edmund Muskie won the Democratic vice presidential nomination. George Corley Wallace's presidential campaign consisted of members of the Ku Klux Klan, John Birch Society, Minutemen, and the American Nazi Party in the South. In the North, the Wallace campaign was supported by the ultra-conservative middle class, factory, and service employers. He ran as a populist. In the North, he had 12 percent in the East and 16 percent in the Midwest. On September 9, 1968, in Philadelphia, Vice President Hubert Humphrey opened his campaign. On Monday, September 30, 1968, in Salt Lake City, Vice President Hubert Humphrey gave a televised speech calling for a complete stop to the bombing of North Vietnam but would continue if the North Vietnamese government did not cooperate in the peace negotiations. On October 31, 1968, at 8:00 p.m., LBJ made a taped appearance on television announcing the bombing stopped. Richard Nixon won 43.4 percent of the popular vote. Vice President Hubert Humphrey won 42.7 percent and George Wallace won 13.5 percent. In the Electoral College, Richard Nixon won 301. He won Florida, South Carolina, North Carolina, Virginia, Tennessee, New Jersey, Ohio, Illinois, Wisconsin, and California. Vice President Hubert Humphrey won New York, Pennsylvania, Michigan, Missouri, and Texas. George Wallace won 34 percent of the popular vote in the South and carried only Louisiana, Mississippi, Alabama, Georgia, and Arkansas. In the North, he only won 8 percent of the popular vote.

During the Nixon administration, the National Environmental Policy Act (NEPA), the Environmental Protection Agency (EPA), the

Controlled Substance Act (CSA), the Endangered Species Act (ESA), and the Roe vs. Wade Supreme Court decision were passed, established, and decided and set the stage for federal policies regarding the environment, drugs, and abortion. During the Reagan administration, the National Minimum Drinking Age Act was passed and set the national drinking age at twenty-one. During the Clinton administration, on February 26, 1993, a Ryder truck containing a bomb detonated under the North Tower of the World Trade Center. Six people were killed. On January 1, 1994, the North American Free Trade Agreement (NAFTA) was formed. On January 1, 1995, the World Trade Organization (WTO) was formed. During the Bush administration, on June 7, 2001, the first of the "Bush tax cuts," the Economic Growth and Tax Relief Reconciliation Act was passed. On Tuesday, September 11, 2001, four hijacked airplanes struck the Twin Towers of the World Trade Center, the Pentagon, and a field in Shanksville, Pennsylvania. 2,996 people were killed. In response to the attacks, the War on Terrorism was declared on October 7, 2001. On October 26, 2001, the US Congress passed the United and Strengthening America by Providing Appropriate Tools Required to Intercept and Obstruct Terrorism (USA PATRIOT) Act. The USA PATRIOT Act is 342 pages long and contains 153 provisions, including money laundering, border protection, computer crime, funding to 9/11 victims, surveillance, information-sharing, etc. On November 25, 2002, the Homeland Security Act was passed. From March 20, 2003, to December 15, 2011, we entered and fought the Iraq War. On May 28, 2003, the second of the Bush tax cuts, the Jobs and Growth Tax Relief Reconciliation Act was passed. During the Obama administration, on February 17, 2009, the American Recovery and Reinvestment Act (ARRA) was passed in response to the Great Recession. The right wing Tea Party Movement began.

The Common Core State Standards Initiative was announced to set up a national public education curriculum in the area of English Language Arts and Mathematics. On March 23, 2010, the Patient Protection and Affordable Care Act (PPACA) was passed. On September 17, 2011, the Occupy Wall Street protests began. On September 11, 2012, the US embassy in Benghazi, Libya was attacked and four Americans were killed. On July 13, 2013, George Zimmerman was acquitted for the murder of Trayvon Martin. The Black Lives Matter Movement was founded. On October 1–16, 2013, the United States federal government shutdown. On April 13, 2015, in Maumee, Ohio, Hillary Clinton stopped at a Chipotle restaurant and ordered a chicken burrito bowl. In May 2015, in Columbia, South Carolina, Hillary Clinton stopped at the Main Street Bakery and met First Calvary Baptist Church minister Donnie Hunt. On June 17, 2015, white supremacist Dylann Storm Roof murdered nine African Americans at the Emanuel African Methodist Episcopal Church in Charleston, South Carolina. Hillary Clinton had just landed in Nevada when she heard the news of the shooting.

On June 26, 2015, the United States Supreme Court ruled in Obergefell vs. Hodges that the Fourteenth Amendment requires states to issue marriage licenses to same-sex couples and to recognize those same-sex marriages that were performed legally out of state. In March 2016, FBI agents met with Hillary for America campaign lawyer Marc Elias and senior campaign staff. In June 2016, Marc Elias got a message from the Democratic National Committee (DNC) that hackers had succeeded in forcing a way into its computer network. On June 14, 2016, the Washington Post told the story. On June 15, 2016, Guccifer 2.0 posted stolen documents. On July 25, 2016, the Democratic National Convention was held in Philadelphia. Speakers were Michelle Obama, Cory Booker, Elizabeth Banks, Anastasia Somoza, Jelani Freeman, Ryan Moore, Lauren Manning, Bill Clinton, Barack Obama, Khizr and Ghazala Khan, Chelsea Clinton, and Hillary Clinton herself. On July 22, 2016, WikiLeaks published twenty thousand stolen DNC e-mails. On July 27, 2016, Donald Trump held a press conference where he said, "Russia, if you're listening, I hope you are able to find the thirty thousand e-mails that are missing." On August 5, 2016, former acting CIA Director Mike Morell wrote an op-ed in the New York Times. On August 8, 2016, Roger Stone told Florida Republicans that he was communicating with Julian Assange and predicted an "October surprise." On August 19, 2016, Paul Manafort resigned. On August 21, 2016, Roger Stone tweeted, "Trust me, it will soon be Podesta's time in the barrel. #Crooked Hillary." In August 2016, Harry Reid wrote a letter to FBI Director James Comey citing Roger Stone's claims and asked for an investigation. On September 5, 2016, the Washington Post reported a "a broad covert Russian operation in the United States to sow public distrust in the upcoming presidential election and in US political institutions." On September 7, 2016, the Commander in Chief Forum was introduced on NBC by Matt Lauer.

On September 26, 2016, at Hofstra University, the first presidential debate was held between Hillary Clinton and Donald Trump. On October 7, 2016, Director of National Intelligence James Clapper and Secretary of Homeland Security Jeh Johnson issued a statement accusing "Russia's senior-most officials of ordering the hacking of the DNC." On October 30, 2016, Harry Reid wrote another letter to FBI Director Comey stating, "It has become clear that you possess explosive information about close ties and coordination between Donald Trump, his top advisors, and the Russian government. The public has a right to know this information." On November 8, 2016, Election Day, at a Chappaqua, New York, elementary school, Hillary Clinton signed her name in a book of voters, checked off her name on the ballot, and put the ballot in the scanner. On November 9, 2016, at 1:35 a.m., the Associated Press called Pennsylvania for Donald Trump. Hillary Clinton called Donald Trump and President Barack Obama. At 2:29 a.m., the Associated Press called Wisconsin and the election for Donald Trump. On January 21, 2017, the day after President Donald Trump's Inauguration, the Women's March on Washington protest was held in Washington, DC. On May 26, 2017, a rainy day in Chappaqua and Boston, Hillary Clinton got dressed in Wellesley blue, had a cup of coffee, and read a note from her husband. She flew to Massachusetts where she met with Wellesley President Dr. Paula A. Johnson on the Wellesley campus. Hillary Clinton put on academic robes and cap in green hall. She talked with Reverend Paul Santmire, Wellesley Republican club president Lauren, and 2017 commencement speaker Tala Nashawati. Hillary Clinton began her speech with "What do we do now? Keep going." On August 12, 2017, at 1:45 p.m., James Alex Fields Jr. drove his car into a crowd of counterprotesters at the Unite the Right rally in Charlottesville, Virginia, at Water and Fourth Streets. He killed Heather D. Heyer and injured nineteen. On December 22, 2017, President Trump signed the Tax Cuts and Jobs Act (Trump tax cuts) into law.

A Theory Explaining Our Current Political Situation

In the section of this book entitled "The Influence of Personality on Politics," I told you "the Parable of the Two Conductors" story. It references the key part of the whole book. This you will need to understand before I go any further. The "steam locomotive" represents the United States federal government. The "fifty cars" represent each of the fifty states, in the order that they came into the Union. The "engineer" represents the president of the united states. The "red jacket conductor" represents the Republican Party and the "blue jacket conductor" represents the Democratic Party. The "left side" of the train represents the left side of American politics, the left side of the House of Representatives and the Senate, Democratic Party–controlled states, etc. The "right side" of the train represents the right side of American politics, the right side of the House of Representatives and the Senate, Republican Party–controlled states, etc. Whenever a major situation occurs, politicians from both political parties will respond by saying, "everything will be all right," meaning that they often give "explanations" that don't make sense or are contradictory. This often results in the people dividing one another and arguing over other less important issues, such as the ones I listed in that section. The leaders themselves, however, divide over which side is better able to handle the situation and should be in control to take care of it. They "bicker and argue" with each other while the situation itself is ignored. The "original terminal" represents when the origins of the two-party politics forming the political foundation of modern America began, which I would say began before, during, and after the Civil War. The "destination of the train and its passengers" represents where the United States and the American people are heading as a result of its two-party politics.

American frontier expansion laid the foundation later on for American foreign imperialism. Thomas Edison, Nikola Tesla, and George Westinghouse each laid the foundation or the electric power industry. John D. Rockefeller laid the foundation for the petroleum industry. Andrew Carnegie laid the foundation for the steel industry. J. P. Morgan laid the foundation for the financial and banking industries. Jacob Riis and Jane Addams laid the foundation for investigative (muckraking) journalists and social workers. The Plessy vs. Ferguson decision in 1896 laid the foundation for half a century of legally enforced segregation in the South and race riots. During William Jennings Bryan's three presidential campaigns in 1896, 1900, and 1908, he established the Democratic Party as pro-silver, anti-imperialist, antibusiness, and prolabor. He was supported by the American Federation of Labor (AFL), the Populist, Progressive, Temperance (Prohibition), and fundamentalist movements. In 1896 and 1900, William McKinley established the Republican Party as pro-nationalist, pro-stability, pro–law and order, pro-business, and pro-imperialist. He was supported by the "big oil, steel, and financial industries." During the McKinley administration, we entered the Spanish-American War and gained control of Cuba, the Philippines, Guam, and Puerto Rico as territories. The anarchist movement inspired Leon Czolgosz to commit his remorseless murder of President McKinley. I place the anarchist movement as a liberal movement along the lines of the revolutionary patriots and the pro-union and anti-slavery abolitionists.

The individualism of the nineteenth-century upper class laid the foundation for the formation of organizations such as the Citizens' Alliances, the National Founders' Association, and the National Association of Manufacturers (NAM). They wanted to protect the interests of the individual business owner by advocating for the open-shop workplace. Under this arrangement, labor unions are excluded and the workers are at the mercy of company management. As introverted as they were, their belief was that the federal government should respond to business by doing nothing. Booker T. Washington was an upper-class African American who advocated that his people submit to white supremacy in order to gain access to white-dominated private universities. He founded the Tuskegee University in Tuskegee, Alabama. African Americans would become independent business leaders alongside whites and segregation would vanish.

The nineteenth-century upper class were the first to own automobiles and were involved in setting up the Preparedness Movement to strengthen the American military during World War I. Their efforts led to the passage of the National Defense Act, the Naval Appropriations Act, the Selective Service Act, the Espionage Act, the Trading with the Enemy Act, and the Sedition Act. These laws provided the basis for the National Security Act, USA PATRIOT Act and the Homeland Security Act. As you can see, the conservative ideology is predominately upper class and introverted, particularly among those involved in the electric power, petroleum, steel, financial, banking, aviation, automobile, and nuclear industries. They are defense contractors that provide material and financial support to the Armed Forces and also form the base of the Republican Party. Upper-class conservatives want themselves and their families to stay in that position in the future. To do that, they must have a child or children to pass down their estates to. Therefore, they are against all forms of birth control, take the pro-life side of the abortion debate, and the "traditional" side of the marriage debate. The American upper class is predominately white and Christian. Therefore, they don't want nonwhites and non-Christians competing with them and they don't want their child or children dating and/or marrying a nonwhite or non-Christian. Therefore, they support a Homeland Security policy that encourages racial profiling, want to restrict immigration to those who can immediately assimilate, such as white Christians. Those of the American upper class only want to pay enough taxes to pay for things that benefit mainly themselves. Defense contractors sell some of their products to the United States Department of Defense, which in turn, buys the former's products. Therefore, American upper-class conservatives want their tax money spent on a large military force and law-enforcement apparatus and want their corporations to run the economy unregulated. A conservative, according to Cambridge Dictionary, is "not usually liking or trusting change, especially sudden change." Therefore, American upper-class conservatives want to assure that things stay as they are and those in the defense industry may go so far as to push for the establishment of a military dictatorship that would dispose of elected leaders and free elections and declare martial law.

The mutualism and support of trade unions by the nineteenth-century working class laid the foundation for the Industrial Workers of the World (IWW/Wobblies), the Women's Trade Union League (WTUL), the Soviet Union, the Communist International (Comintern), the Communist Party of the United States, the Union of Russian Workers (URW), and the National Committee for Organizing Iron and Steel Workers (NCOISW). They wanted to protect the interests of the workers as a whole by advocating for the closed-shop workplace. Under this arrangement, only union members can work at these workplaces and the individual business owner and company management are at the mercy of the workers. As extroverted as they were, they were socialists who believed that the federal government should bring business under public ownership to be used for public interests.

The nineteenth-century middle class and its influence on our current political, economic, and social status will need to be explained in greater detail than the upper and working classes. The American Progressive Movement was initiated by college-educated middle-class women. The nineteenth-century middle-class support of progressivism meant that they were not overly radical like the socialists but were also not stand still conservatives ether. They set out to improve the lives of others, while, at the same time, protecting their own interests. For the purposes of this book, I have divided them into "economic progressives" and "social progressives." For economic progressives, their approach to controlling business was through antitrust laws, regulations, and compensation to society through corporate taxation. As president, progressive advocate Theodore Roosevelt went to work putting these ideas into practice starting with lawsuits against Northern Securities and Standard Oil Company using the Sherman Antitrust Act. Both monopolies were dissolved as a result. On March 2, 1970, 66 years after the federal lawsuit against Northern Securities, the Northern Pacific, the Great Northern, and Chicago, Burlington, and Quincy Railroads merged with the Spokane, Portland, and Seattle Railway to form the Burlington Northern Railroad. On December 31, 1996, the BNR merged with the Atchison, Topeka, and Santa Fe Railway to form the Burlington Northern Santa Fe Railway (BNSF) which now competes with the Union Pacific Railroad. After the federal lawsuit against Standard Oil, the smaller companies became what are today known as ExxonMobil, Chevron, Tesoro, Sunoco, Marathon, and Shell Oil. Whatever couldn't be done with antitrust laws could be done with regulations.

The Interstate Commerce Act established the Interstate Commerce Commission to regulate the railroads. The Pure Food and Drug Act established the Food and Drug Administration (FDA), regulated certain types of drugs and opened the door for future drug prohibition laws, such as the Controlled Substances Act. The Meat-Inspection Act brought the meat-packing industry under control. The Forest Reserve Act allowed the president to set aside wilderness areas as national forests. The Sierra Club promoted this type of conservation, which President Roosevelt supported and established the federal Forest Service to oversee these forests, which today is set at 155. There are also 20 national grasslands. In the 1970s, environmental conservation was strengthened by the National Environmental Policy Act, the Environmental Protection Agency, and the Endangered Species Act. The Newlands Reclamation Act established the Bureau of Reclamation that gives the secretary of the interior the power of eminent domain. This bureau laid the foundation for the New Deal's Tennessee Valley Authority (TVA).

Both of these organizations deal with public works projects and this laid the foundation for progressive policies promoting the use of renewable sources of energy. Regulations were able to bring business under control through consumer protection and environmental laws. However, this wasn't enough.

The economic progressives also had to redistribute the money already accumulated by these corporations and the wealthy individuals who own them. In 1913, the Federal Reserve System was established to bring the banking and financial industries under control and stabilize the currency. The Sixteenth Amendment to the Constitution established the national income tax. The Seventeenth Amendment to the Constitution was an attempt to control corporate influence over the United States Congress by having US Senators elected directly by the people. In 1914, annual incomes were taxed from four thousand dollars to twenty thousand dollars. The Federal Trade Commission was established and the Clayton Antitrust Act was passed. In 1916, income tax rates were raised again and the first permanent inheritance tax was enacted. In 1917, the War Revenue Act was passed and increased taxes further to pay for the American military during World War I. In 1968, the Revenue and Expenditure Control Act was passed and increased income taxes 10 percent on individuals and corporations. The higher these taxes became, the more powerful the federal government became. On the domestic front, it would become a social welfare provider. The United States Housing Corporation (USHC), the Federal Housing Administration (FHA), and the Housing and Urban Development Department (HUD) laid the foundation for public housing projects. The Social Security Administration (SSA), its Medicare-Medicaid amendments, and the Patient Protection and Affordable Care Act (PPACA)'s individual mandate and health insurance exchanges have laid the foundation for a future universal health care system. Alongside controlling business, the economic progressives had to end class conflict between the individual business owner and the workers. They supported Frederick Winslow Taylor's scientific management for this purpose. After it was applied to the workplace, workers were expected to concentrate on being productive and put the interests of society as a whole ahead of their own interests. In 1908, the US Supreme Court decision Loewe vs. Lawlor applied the Sherman Antitrust Act to organized labor. Scientific management would eventually be applied to the public schools where wage cuts (pay deductions) became grade-point losses, temporary layoffs became suspensions, work fines by supervisors became <u>write-ups by teachers</u>, and job dismissals became <u>expulsions</u>. In 1965, the Elementary and Secondary Education Act was passed to provide federal funding to public schools. In 2009, the Common Core State Standards Initiative was established to take the federal government's authority over the public schools from mere funding to actually telling students what they are supposed to know about the world before they graduate. The La Follette-Peters Act, the La Follette Seaman's Act, and the Adamson Act regulated working hours and conditions. This laid the foundation for the establishment of the minimum wage. The Food and Fuel Administrations were established to purchase grain and set the price of coal. This laid the foundation for the Food Stamp program.

The Federal Control Act and the Railroad Administration was established to bring the railroads under the federal government's control. The National War Labor Board (NWLB) and the National Recovery Administration (NRA) not only laid the foundation for business, labor, and government to work together but also set the stage for a future form of corporatism/fascism to take root in the United States. As World War I began, aside from those who supported and actively prepared for battle, there were also those who opposed the war and any involvement with it. These Americans were pacifists who wanted to keep the peace between the United States and other nations by supporting organizations such as the League to Enforce Peace (LEP) and the American Union Against Militarism (AUAM). Although President Wilson did not endorse the latter organization, he too wanted to keep the United States out of the war. His "Peace Without Victory" speech and his "Fourteen Points" statement endorsed a world political, economic, cultural, and social system that laid the foundation for the League of Nations, the United Nations, the anti-Vietnam War Movement, the North American Free Trade Agreement (NAFTA), and the World Trade Organization (WTO). Democratic Party support for strict gun control laws, decreased military spending, and abolishing the death penalty are part of the larger global agenda to "limit the production of firearms and munitions" first proposed by President Wilson. Pacifism is taught in public schools by maintaining a strict, "nonviolent" and "nondefensive" behavioral "code of conduct" for students in order to create a passive labor force.

President Obama and his administration do not refer to the "War on Terrorism" as such but instead as the "Overseas Contingency Operation."

W. E. B. Du Bois was a middle-class African American who advocated that his people end segregation by supporting those of the African American elite. He helped to establish the National Association for the Advancement of Colored People (NAACP) which laid the foundation for the Civil Rights Movement, the 1957, 1964, and 1968 Civil Rights Acts, and the 1965 Voting Rights Act. Martin Luther King Jr. was very much in line with W. E. B. Du Bois and had he not been assassinated in 1968, he would have supported Jesse Jackson in his 1984 campaign for president to carry on the legacy of the Civil Rights Movement. The white economic progressives were not interested in carrying on the Civil Rights Movement's legacy.

What the white economic progressives were, and still are, trying to accomplish through the NAACP, the Civil and Voting Rights Acts, is multiculturalism. Multiculturalism, as defined by Cambridge Dictionary, is as follows: "the belief that different cultures within a society should all be given importance." Therefore, economic progressives support affirmative action programs encouraging multiculturalism, on the path to assimilation. They use Social Security and other social welfare programs to elevate lower-class women from their lower-class status. The women's movement consisted of the Suffrage Movement that laid the foundation in 1920 for the Nineteenth Amendment to the Constitution giving American women the right to vote. The Birth Control League laid the foundation for the Roe vs. Wade Supreme Court decision legalizing abortion as a form of birth control. In the twenty-first century, women are part of the labor force but only a select few have made it to the top executive positions. The majority of women STILL take their HUSBAND'S last name if and/ or when they decide to get married.

The New Deal Coalition established to support FDR laid the foundation for the progressive "liberal" policies of the late twentieth century and twenty-first century Democratic Party. The American

Federation of Labor and Congress of Industrial Organizations (AFL-CIO), the National Education Association (NEA), the Sierra Club, the National Association for the Advancement of Colored People (NAACP), the National Organization for Women (NOW), and the Feminist Majority Foundation make up the "passengers on the left side of the train." They are seeking to elect a president of the United States who will eventually make the Democratic Party the dominant and only political party. Once they accomplish this first step, it is possible that they will start the process of setting up a state capitalist economic system. State capitalism is the whole country governed as one big corporation. The progressive "liberals" want state capitalism on an international scale, bringing every single country under the control of the United Nations. Once the new state capitalist economic system is set up, prisons will play a major role as prisoners will be used as a form of "slave labor." The Thirteenth Amendment to the Constitution states: "Neither slavery nor involuntary servitude, <u>except as a punishment for crime whereof the party shall have been duly convicted</u>, shall exist within the United States, or any place subject to their jurisdiction." Slavery is still allowed in the United States but only in the form of prison labor. The progressive "liberals" are not as "equal" as they want you to think they are. White men are still the majority in both houses of Congress and can still out vote everyone else. Barack Obama is the first African American president but we *still* have a long way to go on racial and gender issues.

The social progressives want to keep immigration confined to those from Northern Europe only through the Chinese Exclusion Act, the Anarchist Exclusion Act, the 1907 Immigration Act, and the USA PATRIOT Act. The American Eugenics Movement sought to "purify" the United States by sterilizing mental hospital patients. It laid the foundation for the Nazi eugenics program. The closest thing we have today that resembles eugenics is the "right to die/physician-assisted suicide" that is allowed only in four states. The Prohibition Movement laid the foundation in 1920 for the Eighteenth Amendment to the Constitution that outlawed alcoholic beverages nationwide. In 1984, the closest thing to prohibition was the National Minimum Drinking Age Act that prohibits those under

21 from drinking alcoholic beverages. The anti-prostitution movement laid the foundation for the White Slave Traffic (Mann) Act that outlawed interstate prostitution in 1910. In 1912, the progressive idea of separating children from the adult world laid the foundation for the federal Children's Bureau. In 1961, the Juvenile Delinquency and Youth Offenses Control Act was passed. The Ballinger-Pinchot controversy laid the foundation for the twenty-first century republican party's anti-environmental and anti-global warming stance.

The Wright brothers laid the foundation for space travel and the aviation industry. Ford and General Motors laid the foundation for the automobile industry. Automobiles became more affordable for farmers, workers, and the middle class. The radio laid the foundation for television, analog and cable networks, and talk-radio. The telephone laid the foundation for the internet. The radio and telephone industries together laid the foundation for the cellular phone industry. The phonograph laid the foundation for the video cassette player, the 8-track player, videocassette recorder (VCR), the compact disc player (CD), iPod, MP3, the digital video disc player (DVD), etc. Albert Einstein's special and general theories of relativity laid the foundation for the construction of the atomic bomb and the nuclear power industry. Modernist art and architecture laid the foundation for modern civilization. William James laid out the methods of modern psychology: analysis, introspection, experiment, and comparison. The publication of "The Mind of Primitive Man" and "The Passing of the Great Race" laid the foundation for racist views of white superiority.

The silent motion picture industry laid the foundation for Hollywood. The Committee on Public Information (CPI) and the Federal Communications Commission (FCC) have regulated Hollywood, analog, and cable networks to the point where the only kind of entertainment that can be presented to the public in the twenty-first century is "propaganda entertainment." The National Board of Review was established to regulate the motion picture industry. Margaret and William Sanger's conviction under the Comstock Act laid the foundation for "pro-life" opposition in the birth control/abortion debate. The Civilian Conservation Corps (CCC) and

Job Corps have laid the foundation for a paramilitary-style police force in the United States similar to the Nazi SS/SA and the Fascist Blackshirts.

The conservative coalition to oppose FDR laid the foundation for the reactionary "conservative" policies of the late twentieth and twenty-first century republican party. The Tea Party Movement is a reactionary American fascist movement. Unlike their conservative allies, fascists are more extroverted and emphasize the collective interests of the group as a whole. But if you're not living your life up to <u>their</u> standards, fascists could care less about you and your problems and more about those who are living up to the "fascist" standard. Chris Hedges defines American fascism as a kind of "religious" movement.

> Dominionism seeks to politicize faith. It has a belief in magic along with leadership adoration and a strident call for moral and physical supremacy of a master race, in this case American Christians. It also has an ill-defined and shifting set of beliefs, some of which contradict each other. The dominionist movement seeks to appropriate not only our religious and patriotic language but also our stories, to deny the validity of stories other than their own, to deny that there are other acceptable ways of living and being. There becomes only one way to be a Christian and only one way to be an American.

The dominionist movement consists of <u>Christian Identity</u>, <u>Pregnancy Services of Western Pennsylvania</u>, <u>Hope for the Heart</u>, <u>Evangelism Explosion</u>, <u>Focus on the Family</u>, <u>Promise Keepers</u>, <u>Engaging Your World</u>, <u>National Association for Research and Therapy of Homosexuality (NARTH)</u>, <u>Illinois Family Institute</u>, <u>Creation Museum</u>, <u>Traditional Values Coalition</u>, <u>National Religious Broadcasters</u>, <u>Family Life Today</u>, <u>Family Research Council</u>, <u>Council for National Policy (CNP)</u>, <u>Center for Christian Statesmanship</u>, <u>Jerusalem Connection</u>, <u>Ohio Restoration Project</u>, <u>World Harvest Church</u>, <u>Trinity Broadcasting Network (TBN)</u>, and the <u>Left Behind</u>

<u>novel series</u>. They believe the United States political, economic, cultural, and social systems should revolve around the Christian religion and be a "Christian nation." The upper-class defense contractors and the Christian dominionites make up the "passengers on the right side of the train." They have elected Donald Trump as president of the United States. President Trump signed Executive Order 13769, the Muslim travel ban. It barred individuals from Iran, Iraq, Libya, Somalia, Sudan, Syria, and Yemen from entering the United States for ninety days, suspended the US Refugee Admissions Program for 120 days, and suspended admission of Syrian refugees indefinitely. Later, President Trump signed Executive Order 13780 to replace 13769. These two executive orders have similarities to Adolf Hitler's Nuremberg Laws, the Law for the Protection of German Blood and German Honour, and the Reich Citizenship Law. President Trump has also appointed Neil Gorsuch and Brett Kavanaugh as Associate Justices of the United States Supreme Court to replace the late Antonin Scalia and retiring Anthony Kennedy. Justices Gorsuch and Kavanaugh are the first step toward the Republican Party's takeover of the Supreme Court and the overturning of Roe vs. Wade and the outlawing of birth control, along with the overturning of Obergefell vs. Hodges and the outlawing of same-sex marriage. President Trump has given into the demands of the upper-class defense contractors by signing into law his "tax cuts." Henry McNeal Turner's International Migration Society and African Methodist Episcopal Church laid the foundation for the 1960s Black Power nationalist movement and the Black Panthers Party, which could be seen as an African American version of fascism. As you can see, the progressive ideology is predominately middle class, particularly among those involved in the operation of the American federal government, state, and local governments. They are the bureaucrats that enforce the laws imposed on the general public and form the base of the Christian fundamentalists and the Democratic Party. Middle-class progressives are the people who enforce our drug laws, environmental laws, trade laws, tax laws, banking laws, finance laws, immigration laws, morality laws, laws concerning children, laws concerning space, nuclear regulatory laws, and censorship laws. They work in our prisons, psychiatric hospitals,

and schools (public and private). The American middle class continuously recruits members of the lower and upper classes to join its ranks to maintain its position in the future. White Christian women and nonwhite non-Christian women, together, make up the majority of American citizens.

In the section of this manifesto entitled, "The Extroverted Personality," I stated that *true* liberals are divided among those who challenge authority, accepted standards, accepted behavior, and traditional values, and those who are simply hostile to all of society. I want to focus on the former. In the Parable of the Two Conductors, when I refer to "you," I am referring to women who are not affiliated with any political party and who are political and nonpolitical leaders in their communities. "Outside the train" represents the international world before and after the United States got involved. "Inside the train" represents the individual personalities of the American people, ranging from loud, obnoxious, and self-righteous to calm, quiet, and orderly. You have a major and necessary role to play in both American society and the world. Your first role is reaching out to female American government bureaucrats. In the Parable of the Two Conductors, I use a steam locomotive as a metaphor for the American federal government. I am trying to show that the American federal government is old, decrepit, and in need of improvement or possibly replacement. The steam locomotive needs a fireman to shovel coal into its boiler to keep its fire burning, the engine running, and the train moving. Coal is, therefore, a source of power for the entire train. Take away the coal and the fire stops burning, the engine stops running, and the train stops moving. Like a steam locomotive, the American federal government relies on civil service bureaucrats, which are like the fireman of a steam locomotive, to enforce its laws, or keep the boiler fire burning, and keep the American federal government operating, or the engine running, and the United States, the train, moving. Just like a steam locomotive, if you take away the civil service bureaucrats, there is no one to enforce the laws of the American federal government, which would then stop operating, and the United States would stop moving. Therefore, in order to stop a dictatorial president of the United States, I am calling for all female employees of the American federal government to go on strike.

1. You will set up a not-for-profit organization and call it the Sisters and Brothers of the United States of America (SBUSA). Its purpose will be to unify American women and supportive American men.
2. The SBUSA will consist of local centers that will function as both refuge and meeting places for SBUSA members.
3. The SBUSA local centers will be placed in every city, town, village, and hamlet across the United States.
4. Each SBUSA local center will be run by a president, vice president, treasurer, and secretary.
5. The SBUSA presidents will be elected by the members of each SBUSA local center. Once elected, the SBUSA president will choose his/her vice president.
6. The SBUSA presidents will make up the SBUSA national committee that will meet once a year in Washington, DC.
7. The SBUSA treasurers will be responsible for collecting the annual membership fee, managing the money, bookkeeping, and etc., for each SBUSA local center.
8. The SBUSA treasurers will be elected by the members of each SBUSA local center.
9. The SBUSA secretaries will be responsible for all records kept at each SBUSA local center.
10. The SBUSA secretaries will be elected by the members of each SBUSA local center.
11. Potential SBUSA members cannot have a felony criminal record.

Female and supportive male members of the SBUSA who are between the ages of twenty-five and thirty will run for seats in the House of Representatives and the Senate.

Female and supportive male members of the SBUSA who are age thirty-five will run for the presidency.

Once elected, members of congress will call an Article 5 constitutional convention to propose amendments to the Constitution:

1. Among the proposed amendments to the constitution will be the direct election of Supreme Court justices' by popular vote.
2. The abolition of the Electoral College.
3. Allowing foreign-born Americans to run for the presidency.
4. Outlawing gerrymandering.
5. Lowering the voting age to sixteen.

SBUSA members will push for renewable energy sources, public housing, a universal health care system, raising the federal minimum wage, improving the Supplemental Nutrition Assistance Program (SNAP) program, getting employers to provide childcare in the workplace, getting more women registered to vote, getting more women to start their own businesses, encouraging more women to keep their own last name if and/or when they decide to get married, getting more women elected to public office, and getting the USA PATRIOT Act and the National Minimum Drinking Age Act overturned. SBUSA members will also push for reforms in the American public school system such as giving students paychecks, end the two-month-long summer break, open the schools on the weekends, replace English language classes with language studies classes, replace state standardized tests, give students the option of going to school part-time, and have K-12 self-defense classes.

BIBLIOGRAPHY / WORKS CITED

Addams, Jane. *Twenty Years at Hull-House*. New York: The MacMillan Company, 1910.

Ashby, LeRoy. *William Jennings Bryan: Champion of Democracy*. Boston: Twayne Publishers, 1987.

Barbeau, Arthur E., and Henri, Florette. *The Unknown Soldiers: Black American Troops in World War I*. Philadelphia: Temple University Press, 1974.

Bellamy, Edward. *Looking Backward: 2000–1887*. 1888.

Brands, H. W. *The Reckless Decade: America in the 1890s* New York: St. Martin's Press, 1995.

Brown, Norman O. *Life Against Death: The Psychoanalytical Meaning of History*. Connecticut: Wesleyan University Press, 1959.

Brown, Norman O. *Love's Body*. New York: Random House, 1966.

Bryan, William Jennings. *The First Battle: A Story of the Campaign of 1896*. Chicago: W. B. Conkey Company, 1896.

Caillois, Roger. *Man, Play, and Games*. New York: The Free Press, 1958.

Chase, Stuart. *A New Deal*. Whitefish: Kessinger Publishing, 1932 (2009).

Chase, Stuart. *Mexico: A Study of Two Americas"* New York: The MacMillan Company, 1938.

Chomsky, Noam. *American Power and the New Mandarins*. New York: Pantheon Books, 1967.

Chomsky, Noam. *The New Military Humanism: Lessons from Kosovo*. Monroe: Common Courage Press, 2002.

Cleaver, Eldridge. *Soul on Ice*. New York: Dell Publishing, 1968.

Clement, Scott, and Green, John C. The Tea Party and Religion. Pew Research Center-Religion and Public Life Project, February 23, 2011.

http://www.pewforum.org/2011/02/23/tea-party-and-religion/.

Clinton, Hillary Rodham. *What Happened*. New York: Simon & Schuster, 2017

Coffman, Edward M. *The War to End All Wars: The American Military Experience in World War I*. New York: Oxford University Press, 1968.

Cohen, Rose. *Out of the Shadow: A Russian Jewish Girlhood on the Lower East Side*. Ithaca: Cornell University Press, 1918.

Connor, Valerie Jean. *The National War Labor Board: Stability, Social Justice, and the Voluntary State in World War I*. Chapel Hill: University of North Carolina Press, 1980.

Conot, Robert. *Rivers of Blood, Years of Darkness: The Unforgettable Classic Account of the Watts Riot*. New York: William Morrow & Company, 1968.

Cooper, Jr., John Milton. *Pivotal Decades: The United States, 1900–1920*. New York: W. W. Norton & Company, 1990.

Diner, Steven J. *A Very Different Age: Americans of the Progressive Era*. New York: Hill and Wang, 1998.

Eischens, Alissa D. *The Dilemma of the Only Child*. Northwestern University.

Fanon, Frantz. *The Wretched of the Earth: A Negro Psychoanalyst's Study of the Problems of Racism and Colonialism in the World Today*. Paris: Francois Maspero, 1961.

Ferrell, Robert H. *Woodrow Wilson and World War I: 1917–1921*. New York: Joanna Cotler Books, 1985.

Fleming, Thomas. *The Illusion of Victory: America in World War I*. New York: Basic Books, 2003.

Flynn, John T. *As We Go Marching*. New York: Doubleday and Company, 1944.

Garland, Hamlin. *Main-Travelled Roads*. Boston: Arena Publishing Company, 1891.

Goldwater, Barry. *The Conscience of a Conservative*. Shepardsville: Publishers Printing Company, 1960.

Goldwater, Barry. *Why Not Victory: A Fresh Look at American Foreign Policy*. New York: Macfadden-Bartell Corp, 1963.

Greenwald, Maurine Weiner. *Women, War, and Work: The Impact of World War I on Women Workers in the United States*. Ithaca: Cornell University Press, 1990.

Haley, Alex (as told to). *The Autobiography of Malcolm X*. New York: Ballantine Publishing Group, 1964.

Harrington, Michael. *The Other America: Poverty in the United States*. New York: The MacMillan Company, 1962.

Hedges, Chris. *American Fascists: The Christian Right and the War on America*. New York: Free Press, 2006.

Howard, Ebenezer. *To-morrow: a Peaceful Path to Real Reform*. New York: Cambridge University Press, 1898.

Huxley, Aldous. *The Doors of Perception*. New York: Harper & Row, 1954.

Jacobs, Jane. *The Death and Life of Great American Cities*. New York: Random House, 1961.

Kazin, Michael. *A Godly Hero: The Life of William Jennings Bryan*. New York: Alfred A. Knopf, 2006.

Kennedy, David M. *Over Here: The First World War and American Society*. New York: Oxford University Press, 1980.

Kerouac, Jack. *Dharma Bums*. New York: Viking Press, 1958.

Kerouac, Jack. *On The Road*. New York: Viking Press, 1957.

King, Jr., Martin Luther. *Why We Can't Wait*. New York: Harper & Row, 1964.

Koistinen, Paul A. C. *Mobilizing for Modern War: The Political Economy of American Warfare, 1865–1919*. Lawrence: University Press of Kansas, 1997.

Kolko, Gabriel. *The Triumph of Conservatism: A Reinterpretation of American History, 1900–1916*. New York: The Free Press, 1963.

Leman, Dr. Kevin. *The Birth Order Book: Why You Are the Way You Are*. Grand Rapids, MI: Baker Publishing Group, 1985

Levin, Jr., N. Gordon. *Woodrow Wilson and World Politics: America's Response to War and Revolution*. New York: Oxford University Press, 1968.

Lillienthal, David E. *TVA: Democracy on the March*. New York: Penguin Books, 1944.

Lofgren, Charles A. *The Plessy Case: A Legal-Historical Interpretation*. New York: Oxford University Press, 1987.

Mailer, Norman. *The Armies of the Night: History as a Novel, the Novel as History*. New York: Plume Printing, 1968.

Marcuse, Herbert. *Eros and Civilization: A Philosophical Inquiry into Freud*. Boston: Beacon Press, 1955.

Marcuse, Herbert. *One-Dimensional Man: Studies in the Ideology of Advanced Industrial Society*. Boston: Beacon Press, 1964.

Matusow, Allen J. *The Unraveling of America: A History of Liberalism in the 1960s*. New York: Harper & Row, 1984.

McCartin, Joseph A. *Labor's Great War: The Struggle for Industrial Democracy and the Origins of Modern American Labor Relations, 1912–1921*. Chapel Hill: University of North Carolina Press, 1997.

McGerr, Michael. *A Fierce Discontent: The Rise and Fall of the Progressive Movement in America, 1870–1920*. New York: The Free Press, 2003.

McMeekin, Sean. *July 1914: Countdown to War*. New York: Basic Books, 2013.

Miller, Scott. *The President and the Assassin: McKinley, Terror, and Empire at the Dawn of the American Century*. New York: Random House, 2011.

Montgomery, David. *Workers' Control in America: Essays in the History of Work, Technology, and Labor Struggles*. New York: Cambridge University Press, 1979.

Oglesby, Carl, and Shaull, Richard. *Containment and Change*. New York: The MacMillan Company, 1967.

Ohlin, Lloyd, and Cloward, Richard. *Delinquency and Opportunity: A Theory of Delinquent Gangs*. New York: The Free Press, 1960.

Parrini, Carl. *Heir to Empire: United States Economic Diplomacy, 1916–1923*. Pittsburgh: University of Pittsburgh Press, 1969.

Paxton, Robert O. *The Anatomy of Fascism*. New York: Vintage Books, 2004.

Persico, Joseph. *Eleventh Month, Eleventh Day, Eleventh Hour: Armistice Day, 1918: World War I and Its Violent Climax*. New York: Random House, 2004.

Rauchway, Eric. *Murdering McKinley: The Making of Theodore Roosevelt's America*. New York: Hill and Wang, 2003.

Riis, Jacob. *How the Other Half Lives: Studies Among the Tenements of New York*. New York: Charles Scribner's Sons, 1890.

Roberts, Stephen Henry. *The House That Hitler Built*. New York: Harper & Brothers, 1937.

Roosevelt, Franklin Delano. *Looking Forward*. New York: John Day Company, 1933.

Schivelbusch, Wolfgang. *Three New Deals: Reflections on Roosevelt's America, Mussolini's Italy, and Hitler's Germany, 1933–1939*. New York: Picador, 2006.

Sharp, Alan. *The Versailles Settlement: Peacemaking in Paris, 1919*. New York: Palgrave MacMillan, 1991.

Smythe, Donald. *Pershing: General of the Armies*. Bloomington: Indiana University Press, 2007.

Soule, George. *The Coming American Revolution*. New York: The MacMillan Company, 1934.

Spencer, Ethel. *The Spencers of Amberson Avenue: A Turn-of-the-Century Memoir*.

Steinson, Barbara. *American Women's Activism in World War I*. New York: Garland Publishers, 1982.

Thurow, Lester. *Generating Inequality: Mechanisms of Distribution in the U. S. Economy*. New York: Basic Books, 1975.

Torr, James D. *The Patriot Act*. Detroit: Lucent Books / Thomson Gale, 2006.

Trask, David F. *The War with Spain in 1898*. New York: The Free Press, 1981.

Turner, Frederick Jackson. *The Significance of the Frontier in American History*. 1893.

Veblen, Thorstein. *The Theory of the Leisure Class: An Economic Study of Institutions*. New York: The MacMillan Company, 1899.

Wexler, Alice. *Emma Goldman: An Intimate Life*. New York: Pantheon Books, 1984.

Williams, William Appleman. *The Tragedy of American Diplomacy*"
New York: W. W. Norton & Company, 1959.

Wolfe, Tom. *The Electric Kool-Aid Acid Test*. New York: Picador, 1968.

Zieger, Robert H. *America's Great War: World War I and the American Experience*. Lanham: Rowman & Littlefield Publishers, 2000.

Alfred Adler's Birth Order. Child development information.com.
Child Development Institute.
Personality Tests. The Big 5 Aspects of Personality.
www.psychometricsuccess.com.
Conservative vs. Liberal Beliefs. 2005.
www.studentnewsdaily.com.

About the Author

Quan Jamel Fort was born on May 21, 1990, in Johnson City, New York. He was raised in nearby Binghamton, New York, by his late mother, Linda Pierce-Fort. As a child and teenager, he and his mother endured domestic abuse at the hands of his mother's boyfriend. He also endured bullying throughout his years in school. He considered many of his teachers to be incompetent. In his senior year of high school, he received a call from a US Navy recruiter and considered joining the Navy. However, he had mild asthma, which was a disqualifier from joining any branch of the US Armed Forces. He also began writing this manifesto.

After he graduated from high school on June 28, 2009, he decided instead to attend SUNY Broome Community College as a business administration major. He soon realized that the only subjects he was interested in were law and politics, which he passed at SUNY Broome. He soon left SUNY Broome to concentrate on this manifesto. But at the beginning of 2016, he realized that he desperately wanted to finish college and get his degree. He also wanted a source of income as he had been unemployed since he stopped selling Avon products in 2012.

He wrote up a five-year plan and started looking for work. He worked two seasonal part-time jobs before being hired part-time at Price Chopper Supermarkets in 2017. During this time, he was also looking for publishers. One after another, they each turned him down. He completed his manifesto in 2017 and submitted it to Page Publishing.